DAVID AUSTIN'S ENGLISH ROSES

DAVID AUSTIN'S ENGLISH ROSES

GLORIOUS NEW ROSES FOR AMERICAN GARDENS

BY DAVID AUSTIN

PHOTOGRAPHS BY CLAY PERRY

Little, Brown and Company
Boston · New York ·Toronto · London

I dedicate this book to my family and all my staff at David Austin Roses, without whom the English Roses would not have been possible

First U.S. Edition

First published in Great Britain in 1993 by
Conran Octopus Limited

ISBN 0-316-05975-7

Library of Congress Catalog Card Number 93-79686

10 9 8 7 6 5 4 3 2 1

Colour illustrations by Gill Tomblin
Line illustrations, pages 83–143, by Valerie Price
Flower arrangements, pages 9 and 70–76, by Shane Connolly (styling by Hilary Robertson)

Americanization: Marjorie Dietz

Consultant Editor: Michael Gibson

Art Director: Mary Evans
Editorial Director: Anne Furniss
Senior Editor: Sarah Pearce
Original Design: Peter Windett
Art Editors: Peter Butler and Simon Bell
Text Editor: Sarah Riddell
Editorial Assistant: Charlotte Coleman-Smith
Production: Julia Golding
Typeset by Servis Filmsetting Limited, Manchester, England
Printed in Italy

CONTENTS

INTRODUCTION

For anyone unfamiliar with the term "English Roses," this is a name I have given to a new race of roses originating in the hybridization of Old Roses from the eighteenth and nineteenth centuries (the Gallicas, Damasks, Portland and Bourbon Roses) with present-day roses (the Hybrid Teas and Floribundas). English Roses were first launched in 1969, although there had been three earlier varieties – 'Constance Spry' in 1961, 'Chianti' in 1967 and 'Shropshire Lass' in 1968 – but these were more in the nature of stepping stones towards the true English Rose. Since that time over eighty varieties have been bred and introduced, and these are now available in many countries. Although English Roses have not as yet received the official recognition of the World Federation of Rose Societies, the international body that rules on the classifications of roses, it is as "English Roses" that they are known – and grown – throughout the world.

I chose the name "English Roses" because I felt that, of all countries, England has always had a special affinity with the rose. The rose has been the symbol of medieval monarchs and modern political parties; it has inspired our poets and found its way into our paintings and designs. We even use the term to refer to a special type of English beauty. Since there were already Scottish Roses and Gallica Roses, why not, I thought, English Roses too? In fact the name has proved to be a success, not only with the English public but also –

Good garden roses bearing fragrant, old-fashioned blooms: such an aim would be worthwhile in itself, but in the English Roses we seek a character that gives them a little extra besides.

something I did not entirely envisage at first – with gardeners of whatever origin.

English Roses have the following characteristics: they combine the form of flower, the fragrance and general character of an Old Rose with the wide range of color and the repeat-flowering – or "remontancy" – of a modern Hybrid Tea or Floribunda Rose; they also retain much of the bushy, shrubby growth of the old varieties. You will find all these characteristics discussed in greater detail in the following pages. It is also worth looking carefully at the photographs throughout this book, because these can sometimes illustrate the differences and similarities between the Old Roses, Modern Roses and English Roses better than I am able to explain in words.

The development of English Roses was carried out at the David Austin Roses nurseries in Shropshire, where the work still goes on today. When I first began some thirty years ago, it seemed to me, as to many others at the time, that the Old Roses had a certain charm and character that had been lost in roses of more recent origin. Certainly, Modern Roses had their own beauties and virtues, but these were of quite a different order to those of their ancestors. Moreover, most Old Roses had a strength and richness of fragrance only occasionally matched by their modern descendants.

The division that had grown up between these two kinds of roses was so wide as to be quite remarkable. As a result, those who now grow roses tend to fall into two quite separate camps – those who prefer Old Roses and those who favor Modern Roses. This is a shame, for most roses have a place in the garden. I have to admit that my own preference leans very much towards the Old Roses, but I recognize that, compared with

The Classification of Roses

When a new group of roses emerges with characteristics sufficiently different from those which have gone before, the subject of rose classification always arises. This topic is much more complex than might at first appear. The ancestry of cultivated roses is now so long and entangled that although categories for the main branches of the rose family have been in use for some time – principally as a guide to the layman in differentiating between them – they are by no means foolproof. There is often no definable border between one group and another and some varieties of rose belong to more than one camp and are therefore impossible to classify.

Much of the confusion lies in the complicated genealogy of the rose. For thousands of years, rose species and the resulting hybrids interbred in the wild (today these species or Wild Roses are comparatively easy to classify as they can be divided up by botanical characteristics). Later, man perfected the techniques of hybridization by hand pollination, but few records were kept of which roses had been used as parents. Our knowledge of the history of the rose must therefore remain incomplete. Nowadays when two roses are crossed, even when the genetic lines are well established, the results are often unforeseen and characteristics of a rose from its long-lost past can make a sudden, surprising reappearance.

Classifying "Modern Shrub Roses," the blanket term now generally applied to most varieties of shrub rose raised after the introduction of the Hybrid Tea in the latter half of the last century, is particularly problematical since this large category of roses embraces an enormously mixed bunch, with few characteristics in common. They can include roses as diverse as Rugosas and tall-growing Floribundas; they can be of almost any size, have double or single flowers, with tall and upright or wide-spreading growth. It is usually only by looking back at a new breed of roses after a lapse of time that it is possible to determine whether its attributes are distinctive enough for it to qualify as a class on its own. While rose breeders ensure that roses keep changing and developing all the time, it is only when rose-growers at large express a consensus of opinion that a genuine new class of rose emerges. Official recognition can then follow.

The soft colors of English Roses produce glorious arrangements for inside the house; this preserving pan contains 'Golden Celebration,' 'The Alexandra Rose' and 'Evelyn.'

Modern Roses, they have two important drawbacks. Old Roses have a very limited spectrum of color, being almost exclusively confined to shades of white, pink, purple and mauve. There are almost no yellows, apricots or other colors of that range and few true crimsons until we come to the Hybrid Perpetuals of the late nineteenth century, which are really the first of the Modern Roses. The second deficiency of the Old Roses is that they flower only once in early summer. With the exception of a few Bourbon and Portland Roses, they produce one magnificent display in the summer months and nothing later. Of course, it is not essential to have repeat-flowering in roses – other flowers bloom only in their season – but for most of us, particularly for those with small gardens, it is highly desirable. The majority of gardeners would not even consider growing a rose that does not repeat.

It was with these thoughts in mind that I set out to develop the English Roses. My idea was to create roses with flowers of old-fashioned cupped or rosette shape and a powerful fragrance, and to combine these virtues with the wide choice of colors and excellent repeat-flowering properties of the Hybrid Teas and Floribundas. At the same time I aimed to keep as much as possible of the essential character or "personality" of the Old Roses, as well as their more natural habit of growth: in short to obtain new Old Roses, if that is not too much of a contradiction in terms. This, in a nutshell, is what English Roses are.

It is not, of course, possible simply to reproduce Old Roses – they have their own genetic make-up which, once mixed with other roses, can never be quite the same again. If we wanted to breed more Gallica Roses, for example, we would have to work exclusively within the Gallica group – a perfectly reasonable thing to do. In fact, I do not wish to create "reproduction" Old Roses; I would greatly prefer the English Roses to be something in their own right. Nevertheless, it is roses that are broadly in the *mood* of Old Roses that I am looking for: roses possessing something of the simple beauty and grace of the old varieties – plus, I hope, a little more besides.

A Long Tradition

The history of the rose stretches back to the dawn of civilization – and beyond – and man's fascination with this plant has continued to the present day. Here, I describe the various groups of roses from the past that we still grow in our gardens, as well as the popular classes of today. Many of these groups, both Old and New, have played a part in the development of the English Roses.

The rose has been with us for as long as we have inhabited the earth, and the evidence suggests that its history predates ours by many thousands of years. The original Wild or Species Rose was a single flower with five (and in one instance four) petals, growing across the continents of the Northern Hemisphere; at some later date double or semi-double forms also appeared. The evolution of the rose was a gradual process that took place over centuries, due at first to natural mutations and later to the ingenuity of man in perfecting the techniques of propagation by hand. In the last hundred years or so, hybridization of roses has advanced at an unprecedented rate. It is even doubtful whether some of our modern Hybrid Tea varieties would be immediately recognizable as roses to our ancestors. To understand how the rose has arrived at its current state – and in particular how this tradition has led to the English Roses – we need to look back at the major branches of the rose "family tree."

'Kathryn Morley' (left) is a charming English Rose, with many of the Old Rose qualities that we have striven to recapture in our breeding program.

The first garden roses occurred probably in the Middle East and then spread by way of ancient Greece and Rome, eventually to be grown all over Europe. The Crusaders of the twelfth and thirteeenth centuries are believed to have brought specimens back with them when they returned from the Holy Land. Whether or not this is true, what is certain is that in the Middle Ages roses were widely cultivated in monasteries throughout Europe. Although they were valued mainly for their medicinal properties, there can be little doubt that they were also highly appreciated for their beauty and fragrance.

These roses were, generally speaking, those to be found in the groups that we now call Gallica Roses, Damask Roses and Alba Roses. All three groups have much in common, with their full, many-petaled, rosette-shaped flowers, shrubby growth and matt foliage – characteristics which can be clearly seen in many of the photographs in this book. Over the centuries new varieties were produced, mostly from chance seedlings. By the eighteenth century gardeners and nurserymen, mainly in France, had started to sow seed for breeding purposes and consciously to select the most desirable seedlings from the progeny. The progress of creating new varieties was therefore greatly speeded up.

At some point between the seventeenth and eighteenth centuries another similar group of roses was added in the form of Centifolias. These were largely developed by French and, in particular, Dutch nurserymen. Like the Gallicas, Damasks and Albas, the Centifolias (literally, "one hundred petals") were beautiful not only in flower but also in growth and, not least, in fragrance. With the arrival of this group the rose became the most prized of all garden flowers – a position which it has held ever since.

The Gallicas are some of the oldest of all roses, and this variety, 'Charles de Mills,' is one of the most beautiful, with a habit of growth typical of its class.

The Gallica 'Tuscany Superb.' Of the original European roses, this and 'Tuscany' (see page 25) come nearest to a true crimson – all the other reds tend towards purple.

GALLICA ROSES

The Gallicas are probably the oldest of these four groups of roses. Long before they received the name by which we now know them, their predecessors were grown by the Greeks and Romans. In 1629 the great English botanist and gardener, John Parkinson, listed twelve varieties. A little later the Dutch began raising seedlings to produce new varieties. It was not long before France also took a hand, and there breeding was carried out on a large scale; and the group that came to be known as Gallicas appeared on the scene. In 1800 there were said to be over a thousand different varieties. Most of these have long since been lost, but there are still more survivors from this group than from any other of this time.

Gallica Roses usually form small shrubs, generally not more than 4ft (1.2m) in height, with strong upright growth and numerous small bristly thorns. Grown on their own roots they will sucker widely, making a dense thicket. The flowers range in color from deep pink to purple, but are seldom clear crimson. They have many petals, forming neat rosette-shaped flowers, but do not have a particularly strong fragrance.

DAMASK ROSES

Like the Gallicas, with which their history runs parallel, the Damask Roses date back to ancient times. They were said to have been widely grown by the Persians and were certainly popular garden plants in the Classical world before being brought to Europe, most probably by the Crusaders. One authority gives credit for this to a Robert de Brie who is said to have carried Damask Roses back to his castle in Champagne some time between 1254 and 1276, when they were distributed throughout France and later found their way to England.

The Damasks are much more elegant than the Gallicas in growth, with open, rather arching branches and long elegant leaves. Their flowers are usually pink and are notable for their rich scent. In fact, they are the chief source in Modern Roses of what we now call "Old Rose" fragrance (see page 45). Both these classes of roses – the Gallicas and the Damasks – play an important role in the parentage of the English Roses.

ALBA ROSES

The third group, the Alba Roses, are of less concern to us here, as so far they have featured little in the breeding of English Roses. They are closely related to the European dog rose (*R. canina*), and are probably the result of natural crosses between this wild rose and Damask Roses. Alba Roses form much larger shrubs than those so far discussed, at one period being known

'Celsiana' is a graceful example of a Damask Rose, with a delicious fragrance and elegant gray-green foliage. It has been in existence since before 1750.

The Alba Rose 'Félicité Parmentier,' with Rambler Roses behind. Most of the Albas that survive rank among the best of the Old Roses. This variety has been in existence since at least 1834.

as Tree Roses. They are particularly beautiful, but hybridize only with great difficulty. Their foliage is a lovely grayish-green color and their flowers are of very soft, clear pink or white.

CENTIFOLIA ROSES

Centifolia Roses, the fourth class in this group, were for a long time thought to include the most ancient of all rose varieties, but recent evidence suggests that they are of much later origin. They have a complex line of development, the work largely of Dutch breeders during a period extending from the early seventeenth

The Centifolias are notable for their sumptuous flowers and fragrance. 'Fantin Latour' has characteristic blooms, with leaves and growth showing traces of China Rose ancestry.

century to the beginning of the eighteenth century. Centifolias have lax, open growth with large and small thorns and big, rounded leaves; the flowers are heavy and often globular in shape, with a great number of petals. Their fragrance is wonderfully rich. These roses have not proved successful for hybridizing, partly because they are very poor producers of seed.

CHINA ROSES

Around 1800, a small group of roses arrived unobtrusively in Britain. These were four China Roses: 'Slater's Crimson China' (introduced in 1792), 'Parson's Pink China' (1793), 'Hume's Blush China' (1809) and 'Parks' Yellow Tea-scented China' (1824). Remarkably little is known about their history. Although the Chinese were notable gardeners, the rose – unlike the the peony and the chrysanthemum – never featured largely in their art or mythology. The China Roses were not particularly spectacular – indeed, they caused hardly a stir at the time – but they did have one property which was to have a great influence on the future breeding of roses: this was the ability to flower repeatedly throughout the summer.

China Roses are very different in character from the original European Roses. They are much lighter in growth, with thin stems and rather sparse foliage giving an airy, twiggy effect. The leaves are darker and more pointed, and often tinged with red when young. In fact, they have the appearance of a more slender version of the Hybrid Tea Rose, although the flowers are little more than semi-double and show almost no sign of the modern pointed bud. They are not particularly hardy and in the British Isles will often grow to no more than 2–3ft (60 or 90cm) in height, although in warm climates they form large shrubs of 6ft (2m) or more.

HYBRID CHINA ROSES

It was not long before the China Roses began to be interbred with the European Roses – probably largely by chance fertilization. The first of these was raised in England in 1815 and known as 'Brown's Superb Blush.' Gradually other hybrids were introduced, resulting in a class of roses that came to be called the Hybrid Chinas. These roses, which are now nearly all lost, followed the pattern of Old Roses in flowering once in early summer. This was due to the dominance of the once-flowering gene of the Old Roses over the remontant or repeat-flowering gene of the China Roses.

As the Hybrid Chinas were interbred among themselves, repeat-flowering varieties started to appear and out of these seedlings came the Portland Roses and the Bourbon Roses. These two classes still retain the form of flower and much of the character of the Old European Roses and have, at least in some degree, the ability to repeat-flower.

PORTLAND ROSES

The Portland Roses are a charming little group; probably no more than a dozen still survive. Their exact origin is very difficult to sort out, but it is safe to say that they have connections with the China Roses, the Damask Roses and the Gallica Roses. They enjoyed no more than a short period of popularity. In 1848 there were eighty-four varieties growing at Kew, but I do not know of any varieties produced after 1860.

The growth of the Portland Roses is short and upright, and in both this and their invaluable ability to repeat-flower we can see a hint of the Hybrid Teas and Floribundas to come. Their flowers and foliage, however, are still indistinguishable in character from that of the original Old European Roses. They have great beauty and a pronounced "Old Rose" fragrance.

Although the Hybrid Chinas have virtually all disappeared, we still have 'Hermosa' (introduced 1840), a very good garden shrub that produces its flowers with remarkable continuity.

BOURBON ROSES

Soon after the appearance of the Portland Roses, another group began to emerge – the 'Bourbon Roses.' They had their origin on the Île de Bourbon, a small island near Mauritius in the Indian Ocean since renamed Réunion. A chance hybrid occurred between the 'Old Blush' China Rose ('Parson's Pink China'), which we still grow in our gardens today, and a variety known as 'Autumn Damask.' These varieties were widely grown on the island and both had the ability to repeat-flower. By good fortune they produced a chance hybrid, which became known as 'Rose Edouard.' A Parisian botanist, one M. Bréon, collected seed from this hybrid, some of which he gave to M. Jacques, gardener to King Louis Philippe of France. From his seedlings M. Jacques raised a variety which he named 'Rosier de l'Île de Bourbon.' This first Bourbon Rose, introduced in 1823, gave rise – no doubt with the help of intercrossing with other roses – to the class we know as Bourbon Roses.

'Louise Odier,' a repeat-flowering Bourbon introduced in 1851. The class represents the link between Old and Modern Roses, with the flower forms of the former, the foliage of the latter.

'Ferdinand Pichard,' an unusual striped Hybrid Perpetual from around 1921, or earlier. The Hybrid Perpetuals and the Tea Roses were the parents of our modern Hybrid Teas.

The Bourbons are quite different to the Portlands, in that they lean towards the China Roses in appearance. In fact, they are the first roses to resemble, both in leaf and growth, our Modern Hybrid Teas. The flowers, however, still retain the shape of the old varieties, but their tendency is, if anything, to be more cupped than rosette-shaped. They also have a rich "Old Rose" scent. Usually taller and more lax in growth than the Portland Roses, they vary in height from 3ft to 5ft (90cm–1.5m). Gradually they overtook the Portlands in popularity, though they appear never to have superseded them.

Hybrid Perpetual Roses

Again overlapping with the Bourbon Roses, we have the Hybrid Perpetuals. These enjoyed great popularity from the middle to the end of the nineteenth century, when they gave way to the Hybrid Teas. I do not regard the Hybrid Perpetuals as true Old Roses, and they have not featured in the breeding of English Roses. A heavier type of rose than any of its predecessors, the Hybrid Perpetual tends to have tall, upright and rather ugly growth. Its flowers often have pointed buds and are exceptionally fragrant. Many of its varieties were of a strong crimson – a color significantly lacking among roses until the Hybrid Perpetuals first arrived on the scene, and one that is often associated with the richest rose perfume (although, ironically, modern red Hybrid Tea varieties often display a disappointing absence of fragrance).

Tea Roses

While the Bourbons were still in fashion, the China Roses had taken another route, largely in France, in the form of a class originally known as "Tea-scented China Roses." The origin of the name is obscure – a reference perhaps either to their scent being like fresh tea leaves or to the tea chests in which they were imported from the East. Tea Roses were the result of crosses between two of the original China Roses – 'Hume's Blush China' and 'Parks' Yellow Tea-scented China' – and possibly later with various Bourbon Roses. The first variety, 'Adam,' was bred in France in 1833 by an English nurseryman of the same name.

The Tea Roses have much in common with the China Roses. They are, on the whole, delicate, both in constitution and appearance, and are subject to frost damage in northern climates, where they have never been widely cultivated. Dainty and beautiful, often with pretty, pointed buds, they have excellent repeat-flowering properties.

HYBRID TEA ROSES

It was by crossing the Hybrid Perpetual Roses with the Tea Roses to give them greater health and vigor that nurserymen in the latter half of the last century gave us the Hybrid Tea Roses. Although these shared a number of features with the Tea Roses, they constituted an entirely new type of rose which quickly came to dominate the gardening scene.

As everyone knows, Hybrid Teas are short, bushy roses with high-pointed buds and flowers in a multitude of different shades of pink, red and yellow; they usually have large, highly polished leaves. They flower freely and continuously and, though intended as bedding roses, are useful garden plants. They are, however, very different from roses of the past – in fact, so different that it would be easy for the uninitiated to regard them as an entirely different species. The Hybrid Teas quickly became so popular that they soon almost completely obliterated the Old Roses, and they remain to this day the most ubiquitous of all garden plants.

FLORIBUNDA ROSES

While the Hybrid Teas were at the peak of their popularity, a new group of roses emerged. These were the Floribundas. For the source of these roses we have to go back to 1875, when the French breeder responsible for the first Hybrid Tea, Jean-Baptiste Guillot of Lyons, introduced two new roses called 'Mignonette' and 'Paquerette.' These were the original varieties of a class that was to become known as Polyantha Roses. They developed from a cross between the extremely robust and hardy climbing species *R. multiflora*, and the repeat-flowering 'Old Blush China' Rose. The Polyanthas inherited the characteristics of both parents: very resilient and hardy, they produce small, Rambler-like flowers in clusters providing a mass of color throughout the summer.

The Floribunda Roses were the result of crossing Polyanthas with Hybrid Tea Roses. The credit for this goes to the Danish hybridist, P.T. Poulsen, who was looking for roses that would thrive in the Scandinavian climate. He crossed the Polyantha Rose 'Madame Norbert Levavasseur' with the Hybrid Tea 'Richmond,' and the result was a rose called 'Rödhätte' or 'Red Riding Hood.' Introduced in 1912, it had small, semi-double, cherry-colored flowers in large clusters. Unfortunately, it seems to have been lost in the turmoil of the First World War and little more has been heard about it since.

After the War, Poulsen's son, Svend, bred and introduced 'Kirsten Poulsen' and 'Else Poulsen,' both of which were a great success. These were followed by other varieties which together formed the basis of the

'Lady Hillingdon' (introduced 1910) is the best of the surviving varieties of Tea Rose, the class that contributed the long pointed bud and Tea Rose fragrance to the Hybrid Tea.

'Alexander,' a Hybrid Tea bred in 1972 from the widely grown 'Super Star' (1960), illustrates the strong colors and high-centered flower shapes characteristic of the Hybrid Teas.

Floribunda class. They retain much of the hardiness, freedom and continuity of flower of the Polyanthas, but have much larger blooms. Sadly, the Polyanthas have no fragrance and the Floribundas very little. Their virtue lies in their ability to produce quantities of bloom throughout the summer, rather than in any particular beauty of the individual bloom.

CLIMBING ROSES AND RAMBLER ROSES

It is remarkable that the rose, which has produced so many beautiful varieties of shrub and bush roses over the ages, should be capable of proving itself in an entirely different direction – as perhaps the finest climbing plant we have. Its development in this field came comparatively late in its long history. Broadly speaking, roses that climb can be divided into two categories – Climbing Roses and Rambler Roses – which are confusing definitions since both are in fact climbing plants.

The Rambler Roses can be described as the climbing counterparts of the Polyanthas and the Floribundas. Again, *R. multiflora* was used as a parent, but also and more extensively *R. wichuraiana*, a very vigorous rose which is more lax and graceful in growth. The two species were again crossed with Tea Roses and Hybrid Tea Roses, but this time large climbers were selected. These were particularly tall and vigorous roses, producing masses of often delicately colored flowers in huge sprays. They are almost never repeat-flowering but provide the most magnificent display early in the summer – a few varieties will produce an occasional second flush of bloom late in the summer. The introduction of these roses cannot be attributed to any single breeder; they mainly appeared in one short burst between 1895 and 1910.

The Climbing Roses have generally larger flowers, held individually or in small sprays. Many are climbing versions of the Tea Roses or of the Hybrid Tea Roses and their many varieties have been introduced alongside the development of their bushy relatives. The most recent addition to the Climbing Roses is a group that has become known as "Modern Climbing Roses."

The Floribundas are free-flowering bedding roses, the result of crossing Hybrid Teas with Polyanthas. 'Arthur Bell' (introduced 1965) is a good, reliable variety.

They are in the main the result of hybridizing a variety of different tall roses with Hybrid Tea Roses. Predominant among the parents of these Modern Climbers is 'New Dawn,' a sport of the very tall and robust Wichuraiana Rambler 'Dr W.Van Fleet.' 'New Dawn' is almost identical to its parent, except that it has the ability to repeat-flower. Moreover, although it grows quite tall, it does not, owing to its remontant habit, reach anything like the height of 'Dr W.Van Fleet.' 'New Dawn' has been largely responsible, however, for the development of the truly repeat-flowering race of Modern Climbing Roses.

NOISETTE ROSES

This group of Climbing Roses, which stands somewhat apart from other climbers, was originally the result of a cross between the Musk Rose (*R. moschata*) and 'Parson's Pink China.' The cross occurred in the early

1800s in Charleston, South Carolina, and was named 'Champney's Pink Cluster' after its breeder. Philippe Noisette, a nurseryman also of Charleston, sowed seed from this rose which resulted in 'Blush Noisette,' a variety that is still widely grown today. 'Blush Noisette' has the prized repeat-flowering gene and was the first recurrent Climbing Rose. Noisette Roses have played an important part in the breeding of English Roses, particularly through the famous old variety 'Gloire de Dijon' introduced in 1853.

Hybrid Musks, Rugosas and Modern Shrub Roses

These three groups, all developed in the twentieth century, include some excellent garden shrubs, some of which are repeat-flowering and others not. They have had, however, only a very indirect influence on English Roses. In spite of their name, the Hybrid Musks are only remotely related to the Musk Rose. They bear large sprays of usually double flowers on tall, graceful growth, rather like a refined Floribunda Rose. The best varieties were nearly all bred between 1900 and 1930 by the Revd Joseph Pemberton of Essex.

The Rugosas are all hybrids of the species *R. rugosa*, which grows in China and Japan. They are excessively hardy and robust, with large rough-textured leaves and many strong thorns. The wild species is unusual in that it is naturally repeat-flowering throughout the summer. The blooms are large and single and have an almost papery appearance. The species has passed on many of its qualities to its hybrids, which have flowers of rather Old Rose appearance – sometimes with a strong fragrance. Like the Hybrid Musks, these also were largely bred in the early part of the century, although there has been a steady trickle of new varieties since that time. Rugosa hybrids have been used in the breeding of a few English Roses.

Modern Shrub Roses, the result mainly of crossing Modern Hybrid Teas and Floribundas with a wide variety of different Species, form a large and diverse group. They produce large garden shrubs, usually with flowers of "Modern" appearance, while retaining the robust natural growth of their Species ancestor.

The Revival of the Old Roses

From this short survey of the main classes of the rose, the reader might get the impression that as one class of roses led to another, all others faded away. Up to the time of the Hybrid Teas, this was not the case. Rose books of the late nineteenth century describe all the various groups living quite happily alongside each other, though as time went by a new class might become more fashionable than those that preceded it. Only with the arrival of the extraordinarily successful Hybrid Tea did the earlier varieties begin to disappear. If we look at rose specialists' catalogues of the 1920s and 1930s we find no more than three or four varieties of the Old Roses lurking towards the end. Of the many thousands of old varieties, almost all appear to have vanished without trace.

Fortunately, all was not lost. Not long after the apparent demise of the beautiful Old Roses, various discerning collectors started to scour gardens for surviving examples and to hoard them in their gardens. It was at this time that these roses first began to be known as "Old Roses." Extensive collections were built up, and by the 1950s Graham Thomas, the leading authority on old-fashioned roses, had consolidated them all into one large collection, first at Hillings & Co. of Woking, England, and later at Sunningdale Nurseries. From there, the roses soon found their way to all parts of Britain and eventually to other countries and the new cult of Old Roses came into being. Since then other varieties that were thought to have disappeared entirely have been – and are continually being – discovered in various parts of the world.

Today we have two great traditions of the rose existing side by side: the Old Roses, with their taller, shrubby growth and flowers that open wide in a variety of shapes from deep cups to flat rosettes, and the so-called Modern Roses, with their dazzling array of colors, high-pointed buds, short upright growth and shiny leaves. Whereas Modern Roses are often, but not always, fragrant, they cannot compare with the strength and richness of scent of the Old Roses – a quality which we have been able to reintroduce, I believe successfully, into the English Roses.

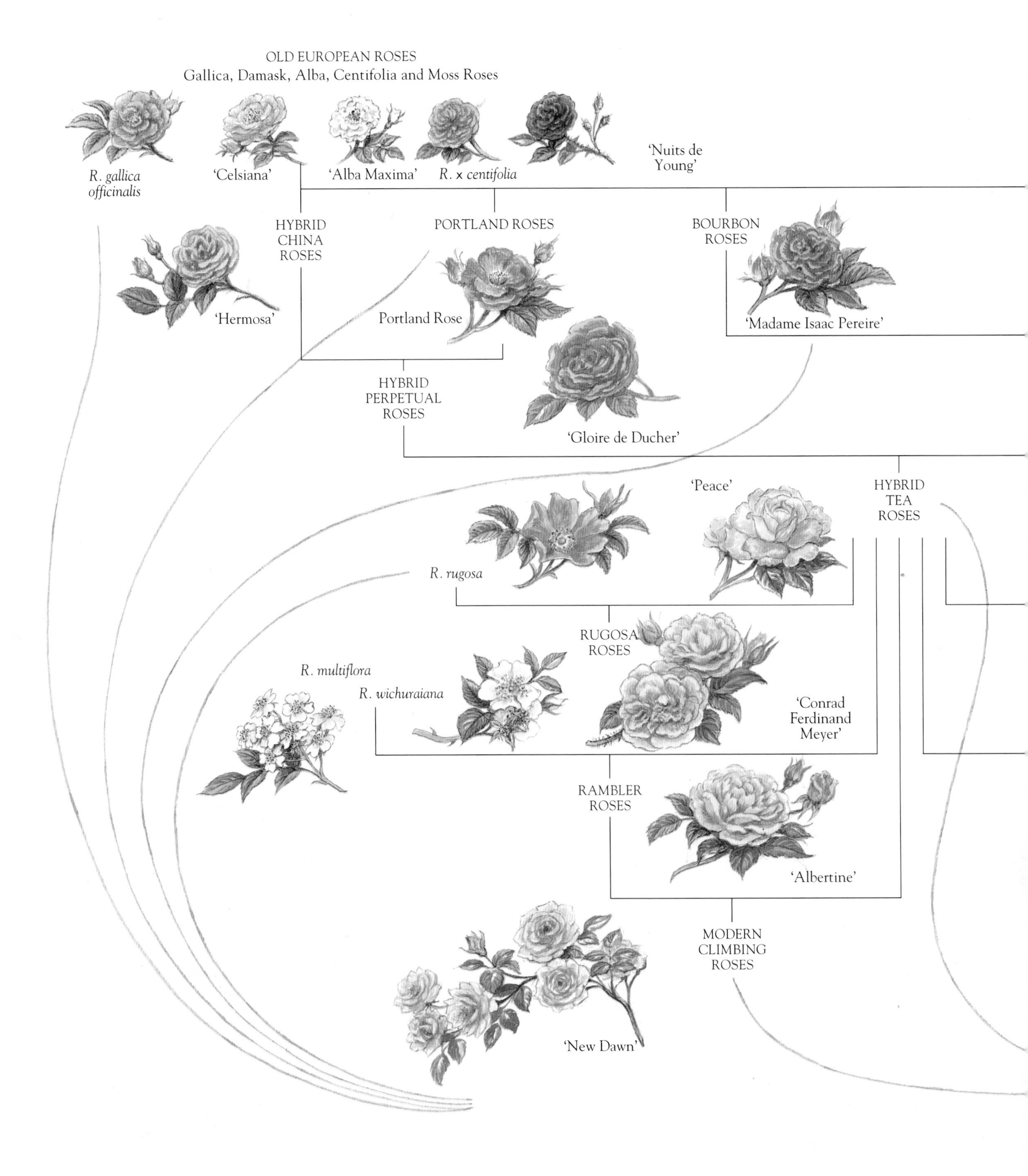

OLD EUROPEAN ROSES
Gallica, Damask, Alba, Centifolia and Moss Roses
R. gallica officinalis
'Celsiana'
'Alba Maxima'
R. x centifolia
'Nuits de Young'
HYBRID CHINA ROSES
PORTLAND ROSES
BOURBON ROSES
'Hermosa'
Portland Rose
'Madame Isaac Pereire'
HYBRID PERPETUAL ROSES
'Gloire de Ducher'
'Peace'
HYBRID TEA ROSES
R. rugosa
RUGOSA ROSES
R. multiflora
R. wichuraiana
'Conrad Ferdinand Meyer'
RAMBLER ROSES
'Albertine'
MODERN CLIMBING ROSES
'New Dawn'

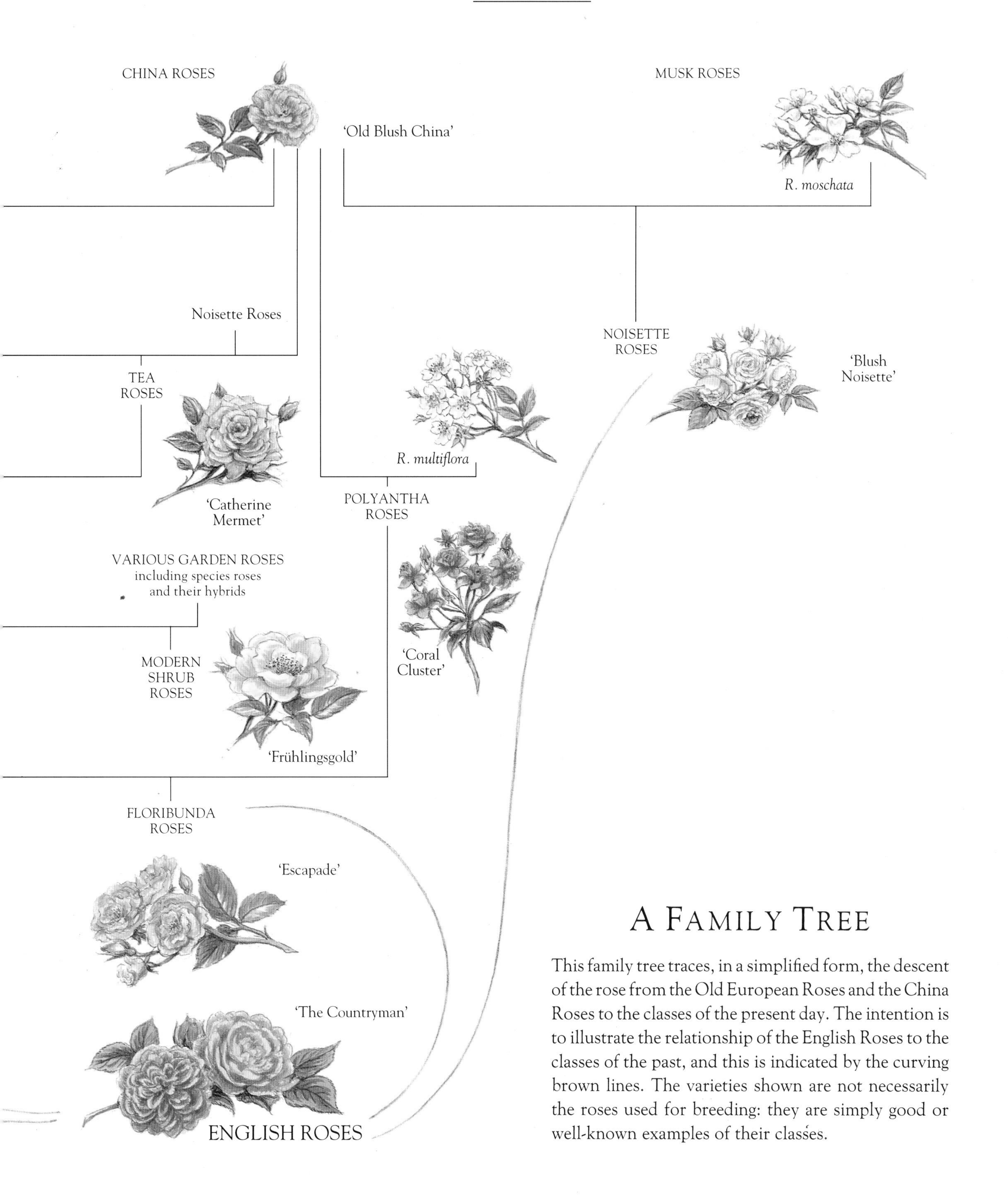

A FAMILY TREE

This family tree traces, in a simplified form, the descent of the rose from the Old European Roses and the China Roses to the classes of the present day. The intention is to illustrate the relationship of the English Roses to the classes of the past, and this is indicated by the curving brown lines. The varieties shown are not necessarily the roses used for breeding: they are simply good or well-known examples of their classes.

The Old and the New

My first attempts at rose hybridization were tentative and experimental; but it soon became clear that it was possible to combine the beauty of the Old Roses with the practical virtues of the Modern – to blend the old with the new. Here I trace the descent of the English Roses from their early beginnings to the many varieties of today.

When I started experimenting with hybridizing roses in the 1940s and 50s, I was aware that the sophisticated breeding techniques of previous years had undoubtedly given us an astonishing diversity of roses. Nonetheless, it was clear that the Old Roses and the Modern Roses had come to represent two quite separate traditions. When I considered these two types of roses, it soon became obvious that both had qualities which suggested that a marriage between the two would be desirable. I believed that if we could take chosen factors from each, a rose might be born that in the course of time could become superior to both. What we had to do was to select Old Roses of outstanding beauty and fragrance, and to cross them with Hybrid Teas and Floribundas for their reliable repeat-flowering and array of colors; if the latter already showed a touch of the character and fragrance of an Old Rose, so much the better.

'Mary Rose' (left) includes, via English Rose parents, Gallica, Hybrid Perpetual, Hybrid Tea and Floribunda in its make-up. An excellent garden shrub, it is an ideal marriage of old and new.

I should perhaps explain here that almost all new roses are produced by a process of "hybridization" – that is, the rose breeder transfers pollen from one variety to another to produce seed. When the seed is sown each of the resulting seedlings will have a mixture of the characteristics of its two parents, and every one will be unique. Seedlings are usually produced in large numbers; it is the selection of an outstanding example that provides the new rose. For those readers interested in the methods of propagation used in our Shropshire nurseries, further details are given in Creating a New Rose (pages 152–7).

A Marriage of the Old and New

Not long after the Second World War I bought a bush of 'Stanwell Perpetual' from the famous nursery of Bunyards in Kent, where Edward Bunyard had gathered together the first small collection of Old Roses. This Scottish rose is unique in its class, in that it is

repeat-flowering. This is almost certainly due to it being a chance cross between R. *spinosissima* and a Portland Rose. 'Stanwell Perpetual' bears double blush-pink blooms of slightly ragged but beautiful Old Rose appearance. It is otherwise indistinguishable from any other Scottish species hybrid, having typical small, fern-like foliage and shrubby growth. To me, the most striking features of this rose were its clear, soft pink coloring and delicious fragrance. It occurred to me then that if this rose could simply happen by chance, there was really no reason why the once-flowering Old Roses should not be hybridized with the repeat-flowering Modern Roses to similar effect.

When I first decided to put my ideas to the test, I cannot say that I proceeded with any great degree of planning. For one thing, my knowledge of Old Roses at the time was very limited. Moreover, I was simply an amateur dabbling in hybridization. For my first parent roses I chose varieties that seemed to me to have the most desirable qualities. Today I might have gone about it differently, but luck must have been on my side and, in hindsight, I do not think I could have made a better choice.

The first Old Rose parent that I selected was the attractive little Gallica 'Belle Isis.' Bred by Parmentier of Belgium and introduced in 1845, this short, twiggy, bushy shrub grows to no more than 3ft (90cm) in height. It has quite small flowers of very soft pink which are tightly packed with numerous short petals forming a rosette of the utmost delicacy and charm. It is also very tough and reliable. I crossed this Old Rose with the excellent Floribunda 'Dainty Maid,' bred by E.B. Le Grice in 1938 and very popular at the time. This

The Gallica 'Belle Isis' (top left) and the Floribunda 'Dainty Maid' (top) became the parents of the first English Rose, 'Constance Spry' (above). This rose has the advantage of growing exceptionally strongly, although it flowers once only.

repeat-flowering Modern Rose, still to my mind one of the most beautiful of its class, forms a tough bush with stout stems and large foliage. Its flowers are single and clear pink in color, opening wide to show their golden stamens. It, too, is a most reliable rose.

THE FIRST ENGLISH ROSES

Out of the seedlings from this cross there appeared one that stood out from all the rest. This was the rose that is now known as 'Constance Spry.' The surprising thing was that, unlike either of its parents, it turned out to have exceptionally large cupped flowers of almost peony-like proportions. These magnificent blooms, indistinguishable from those of an Old Rose, have silky petals of clear pink and a strong fragrance of myrrh (see

The Gallica 'Tuscany' (top) and the Floribunda 'Dusky Maiden' (introduced 1947; top right) gave us 'Chianti,' the founding red English Rose. The flowers of this fine shrub fade to a rich purple as they age, as illustrated here. It is vigorous but once-flowering.

page 44). It forms a large sprawling shrub of great vigor which, when planted against a wall or other support, will also grow into a fine climbing rose. 'Constance Spry' was introduced in 1961 by Sunningdale Nurseries – our nursery had not as yet been brought into being – and was the main foundation rose in the future development of the English Roses.

Whenever a repeat-flowering rose is crossed with a once-flowering rose, as with the parents of 'Constance Spry,' the resulting seedlings will nearly always be once-flowering. In other words, the repeat-flowering gene is what is known as "recessive." To overcome this, 'Constance Spry' had to be 'back-crossed' at least once more with a repeat-flowering rose to ensure recurrent-flowering characteristics. Only then could I be confident of getting a small proportion of repeat-flowering seedlings. One of a number of different roses I chose for this was a Floribunda called 'Ma Perkins,' bred by Boerner and introduced by Jackson and Perkins in 1952. This rose had two advantages: first it was known to produce plenty of excellent seed that germinated well (an important factor in rose breeding), and second it was one of the few Hybrid Tea and Floribunda Roses that had flowers of Old Rose appearance. These were distinctly cupped in shape, rather like a Bourbon Rose. With 'Ma Perkins' I was hopeful that the Old Rose characteristics of 'Constance Spry' would not be lost in future generations. As I anticipated, these crosses produced some repeat-flowering seedlings. By crossing these together, and with Modern Roses, I was able to produce a small group of roses with Old Rose flowers that were reliably recurrent. To reach this point had taken eight years.

The early pink Hybrid Tea 'Mme Caroline Testout' was another rose that I used at this time. It was bred by the French firm of Pernet-Ducher and introduced in 1890. Like 'Peace' in the early part of the twentieth century it, too, was very hardy and reliable and planted in vast quantities. Like many other Hybrid Tea Roses of its time, 'Mme Caroline Testout' retained much of the look of an Old Rose, being globe-shaped with numerous petals. From crosses with this rose I obtained 'Wife of Bath,' a pretty little rose with attractive cupped flowers of pure rose pink, and in turn a good parent. More crosses with 'Constance Spry' gave me further varieties. I still had only pink roses, but their color was exceptionally pure.

Meanwhile I was trying to breed good red varieties. My first real success was with 'Dusky Maiden,' another Le Grice Floribunda, and similar to 'Dainty Maid' in every respect except for its deep crimson coloring. By crossing 'Dusky Maiden' with the deep crimson-purple Gallica Rose 'Tuscany,' I obtained the beautiful 'Chianti.' Introduced in 1967, also through Sunningdale Nurseries, this was the red counterpart of 'Constance Spry.' It has large crimson-purple flowers of Old Rose appearance and a wonderful fragrance. 'Chianti' forms a large shapely shrub but, like 'Constance Spry,' flowers only once in summer. Again, I back-crossed this rose, this time with various red Modern Roses. Unfortunately, nearly all the resulting seedlings turned out to be rather weak. So I looked to the excessively vigorous Shrub Rose 'Gipsy Boy,' with its fragrant, deep crimson-purple flowers of Old Rose appearance. Its only known disadvantage was that it had only one flowering season in early summer. Having crossed this rose with some of the seedlings from 'Chianti,' I was surprised to find that the first generation roses were repeat-flowering. This indicated that 'Gipsy Boy' itself must have had at least one repeat-flowering ancestor.

The best seedling from the union of 'Gipsy Boy' and 'Chianti' was a rose we named 'The Knight.' This rose had very weak growth, but attractive flowers of a lovely rich crimson coloring. We crossed it with the early Hybrid Tea 'Château de Clos Vougeot,' a rose known to produce a deep crimson coloring, and the result was 'The Squire.' This rose, with its magnificent crimson flowers, still left much to be desired in its growth, but has proved an excellent parent, and has been responsible for most of our best red varieties.

By 1969 I had a small range of roses ready to be launched. These roses were so different from any others at the time that it would have been unreasonable to expect commercial nurserymen to grab them with both hands and include them on their lists. As I had always been a farmer, I was in the fortunate position of being able to grow the roses myself. So in 1970 I formed a nursery called 'David Austin Roses' in order to introduce my English Roses to the public. The first varieties included 'Wife of Bath,' 'The Prioress' and 'Canterbury,' as well as three others that have since been deleted – 'The Yeoman,' 'The Knight' and 'Dame Prudence.' It was a slow start, but before long gardeners began to show a small but increasing interest.

'Iceberg' (introduced 1958) is one of the best Floribundas. As a founding parent of the 'Heritage' strain, it has influenced some of our strongest varieties, including 'Graham Thomas.'

NEW LINES

At this point in our breeding programme, we still had problems. In our search for small- to medium-sized Shrub Roses of robust, healthy growth and graceful arching or bushy habit, we had always chosen vigorous parents. In spite of this, the resulting seedlings were not generally as strong as we would have liked them to be. One of the unpredictable features of rose breeding is that it is possible to take very vigorous parents of widely varying type, and produce progeny that is itself anything but vigorous. Another consideration was that we still had no yellow shades. We therefore looked around for parents that might be able to improve our roses and extend our range.

One line that was to have a marked influence on the English Roses was based on the white Floribunda 'Iceberg.' This very familiar rose, bred by Kordes of Germany in 1958, is one of the best of its class. As a hybrid of the Hybrid Musk Rose 'Robin Hood,' it might more accurately be described as a small Shrub Rose. It is exceptionally repeat-flowering and often continues flowering late into the winter. Though not impressive in themselves, the flowers are plentiful and held in attractive sprays; in the autumn they take on a different appearance, often turning a blush-pink shade and looking very much like those of a small Old Rose. With its broad, bushy and dense growth, it seemed to me to have many qualities that could be of benefit to the English Roses.

The first results from crosses between 'Iceberg' and certain English Roses yielded a rose that was probably the most beautiful we had produced up to that time. Its flower was a perfect, soft pink rosette of superior Old Rose appearance. The great disappointment was that it had one failing – it suffered, like 'Iceberg' but to a much greater degree, from blackspot and so could not be marketed. We therefore back-crossed this rose with some of the better English Roses and came up with a handful of our finest varieties of that time, including 'Heritage' and 'Perdita' – two roses notable for their resistance to disease. Today we would probably never have bred from this seedling for fear of producing further susceptibility to blackspot.

Still in search of strength and health, we turned to the Climbing Rose 'Aloha.' This rose was bred from 'New Dawn,' which is generally regarded as one of the most disease-resistant of all garden roses. 'Aloha' is more of a short shrub than a Climbing Rose – it is as a

'Heritage' was introduced in 1984. Like its grandparent 'Iceberg,' (left) it forms an excellent garden shrub, with graceful, bushy growth and strongly fragrant flowers.

The beautiful Noisette Rose 'Gloire de Dijon' is one of the few yellow Old Roses. It has been an invaluable parent to some of our best varieties of English Roses.

shrub that we recommend it to our customers – and it has two other excellent qualities apart from its great vigor: its flowers are of true Old Rose formation and they are extremely fragrant. Its strength was, however, the specific virtue that we wished to pass on to our roses. This we were able to do successfully and a number of very vigorous fragrant varieties from 'Aloha,' including the strong-growing, apricot-yellow 'Charles Austin,' were produced as a result.

The third line we pursued was by way of the Rugosa hybrid 'Conrad Ferdinand Meyer.' At first we harbored no great hopes of success, for we feared that the resulting seedlings from a cross with this excessively vigorous hybrid would be altogether too gross in character. 'Conrad Ferdinand Meyer' was itself a cross between the very popular and beautiful Climbing Noisette Rose 'Gloire de Dijon,' and an unknown Rugosa hybrid. It also had one of the most powerful and delicious fragrances. As before, we crossed this rose with some of our better English Roses at that time, in particular 'Chaucer,' and had one of those pieces of luck that sometimes turn up in rose breeding. Some of the seedlings from this cross were of typical Rugosa appearance, while others bore absolutely no resemblance to a Rugosa Rose. It seemed that some of our hybrids had taken the genes only from the 'Gloire de Dijon' half of 'Conrad Ferdinand Meyer,' while others had inherited those from the Rugosa side. What we had in many instances were in effect hybrids of 'Gloire de Dijon.' They had a lovely rosette shape, with good, silky petals, unusually large in size, and a wonderful fragrance. It was these hybrids which, in future generations, were to give us some of the most beautiful yellow and apricot-colored English Rose varieties that we have bred, including 'Jayne Austin' and 'Evelyn.' Plant breeders often make progress by good luck; the art lies in recognizing it when it appears.

Among many of the most influential characters in the descent of the English Roses through their generations, one rose deserves particular mention. Although sadly the record of its breeding has been lost,

'Charles Austin' shows the influence of 'Aloha' on the English Roses. It has in turn passed on its sumptuous form of flower to such progeny as 'Golden Celebration.'

'Sharifa Asma' is one of the many beautiful descendants of 'Mary Rose,' but with finer flowers and shorter growth. The Damask Rose 'Celsiana' is in the background.

'Mary Rose' is in many ways the ideal English Rose. It has a good, compact, shrubby and twiggy growth, excellent resistance to disease and it repeat-flowers remarkably well. The flowers do not have an overwhelming fragrance, but in every other way I consider it the perfect garden rose. We have been able to cross 'Mary Rose' with many roses to produce some excellent shrubs, including 'Sharifa Asma' and the charming 'Kathryn Morley.'

Other successful parents have also included Old Roses such as 'Duchesse de Montebello' and other Gallicas, the beautiful Portland Roses, particularly 'Comte de Chambord,' and some of the Bourbons that already have so much in common with the English Roses. On the "Modern" side we have used the Floribunda 'Chinatown' and the short Climber 'Parade,' as well as many others. Later generations are the result of crosses between existing English Roses, and I expect it is largely in this direction that we shall make progress in future. Breeding new roses is inevitably a matter of trial and error – as well as requiring great patience – and as often as we have had our successes, we have found ourselves up a blind alley.

The result of drawing on such a diversity of parents is that we have not just one type of English Rose, but a great range of different strains. We welcome this, since it adds to the interest of this group of roses in general and to their individual beauties in particular. Each strain has its own character of flower, foliage and growth and I believe that these differences should be maintained. Examples of each strain are illustrated on the following two pages.

THE STRAINS OF ENGLISH ROSES

It is helpful to categorize the majority of English Roses into eight broad strains – although the divisions are somewhat arbitrary, since every variety is individual.

1 "OLD ROSE" STRAIN

These are roses of strongly "Old Rose" character of flower, which do not fit easily into the other seven groups listed here. They are often original crosses, such as 'Chaucer,' 'Constance Spry' and 'the Reeve.'

2 'HERITAGE' STRAIN

Related to the Floribunda 'Iceberg,' these roses include such excellent varieties as 'Heritage' itself, 'Perdita' and 'Graham Thomas' (illustrated above). They tend to have short, rather shiny leaves, good bushy growth and usually a "Tea Rose" fragrance.

3 'MARY ROSE' STRAIN

Usually with pleasing bushy growth and good repeat-flowering, examples of this strain include 'Mary Rose' (illustrated), 'Charles Rennie Mackintosh,' 'Redouté' and 'Winchester Cathedral.'

4 'WIFE OF BATH' STRAIN

With much of the character of the original Gallica parent, 'Belle Isis,' these are usually short, bushy and tough, with "Old Rose" appearance and good "myrrh" fragrance. Here we have varieties such as 'Wife of Bath' (illustrated), 'Emily,' 'Ambridge Rose,' 'Sharifa Asma,' 'Glamis Castle' and 'Cottage Rose.'

5 'PORTLAND' STRAIN

These would be quite at home with the Portland Roses, with which they have strong affiliations. They have long, rather drooping Damask Rose leaves coming right up to the flower, and a rich "Old Rose" fragrance. At the time of writing, there are two varieties: 'Gertrude Jekyll' (illustrated) and 'The Countryman.'

6 'GLOIRE DE DIJON' STRAIN

Related to the famous old Noisette Rose of that name, and through it back to the Tea Roses, these have rather "modern" leaves and large, lustrous flowers, often in apricot and yellow shades. They include 'Evelyn' (illustrated), 'Jayne Austin' and 'Sweet Juliet,' all of which have something of the "Tea Rose" fragrance.

7 'ALOHA' STRAIN

These are descended from the Modern Climbing Rose 'Aloha,' and have strong, bushy growth and rather heavy flowers of true Old Rose character. In this strain we have 'Charles Austin,' 'Abraham Darby' and 'Golden Celebration' (illustrated), all very fragrant.

8 'THE SQUIRE' STRAIN

Related to 'Chianti' and 'Gipsy Boy,' these include most of our red and crimson varieties. They tend to be of a rich, dark color and have stout, prickly growth and a very strong "Old Rose" scent. Red roses are notoriously difficult to breed, but this strain includes some admirable varieties, such as 'L.D. Braithwaite' (illustrated) and 'The Dark Lady.'

The Ideal of an English Rose

For a rose to qualify as an English Rose it must conform to certain criteria – the shape of its flowers, the richness of its scent, a natural habit of growth and, above all, a certain charm or appeal, drawn from its Old Rose ancestry but that is nonetheless its own. Together, these are the characteristics that set English Roses apart from other Modern Roses.

In breeding English Roses I have always had in mind a picture of how I would like them to be. So far I have given only a general description of their qualities, with a few particular examples to illustrate the story as it has developed. Here I would like to discuss English Roses in greater detail and to say something of the criteria which have guided their breeding and of my hopes for them in the future. For to me, this is the most important issue of all: if the English Roses are to become a class in their own right – and not just another Modern Shrub Rose – they must display a distinctive character and make a unique contribution to the great genus of the rose.

The basic principles that combine to make up the ideal English Rose are outlined below. They include beauty of form, purity of color, pleasing natural growth, attractive foliage and strong fragrance. This last quality adds another dimension to the rose, and is one I regard of such importance that I have allotted the subject a chapter of its own (see pages 43–7). Other characteristics, such as reliability and health, must also be present, and it is the combination of qualities that

Opposite, celebrating the English Rose with the three recent varieties 'Glamis Castle' (center top), 'Evelyn' (left and right), and 'Redouté'. Above, 'Wise Portia.'

determines the nature of an English Rose. It is not enough, for example, that English Roses should produce blooms of vaguely Old Rose shape. It would not be difficult to visualize giant, blowsy, brightly colored flowers such as these, with no particular virtue other than their sheer size and brilliance. Such roses would be very easy to breed, and this has indeed been the fate of a number of other popular garden flowers. We could soon find ourselves going down this path before we were really aware of it. What we need to discern is the essence of the rose – the special qualities that have given the rose its unique place in our hearts down the centuries. This is what we have to distill, as best we can, in the English Roses.

FORM OF FLOWER

The first thing you notice about the English Roses is that their form of flower is entirely different to that of other roses of the present day. In the Hybrid Teas, and indeed in most Floribundas, the beauty of the flower lies in the unfolding bud. Such flowers are most attractive, but their beauty is short-lived: as soon as the bud opens we are left with a flower that is usually little more than a formless muddle of petals. Breeders have developed the high-pointed bud to such an extent that it is no longer possible for it to open out into a flower of any recognizable shape.

Over the many thousands of years of evolution of garden roses such a form of flower was unknown. It is only in the last 150 years that flowers like this have become fashionable. All the Old Roses before then had blooms that were open, such as we find in the peony or carnation. The English Roses therefore mark a return to this form. The flower of an English Rose may also be beautiful in the bud, though it is not usually "scrolled," as is the case in the Hybrid Tea. It is generally more in the nature of a pretty, small cup. The flower gradually opens in a succession of appealing stages until it is completely open – and only then is its full splendor revealed. It will hold its beauty for some time, for as the outer petals die, the inner petals remain fresh. English Roses have comparatively long-lasting flowers – making them very suitable for cutting (see page 71).

The basic shape of an English Rose is a "rosette" – the form that the rose first evolved when it was developed from a wild species into a garden rose by the doubling of its petals. Such doubling is due to the fact that the stamens of all kinds of plants, not only of roses, frequently mutate naturally into petals. The term "rosette," meaning "like a rose," may seem an odd one to apply to roses, but it does show how far the Modern Rose with its high-centered flower has deviated from the rose's original form. A typical rosette can take on many forms (see opposite): it may be closely packed with small petals, for example, or more loosely packed, perhaps with larger petals.

In some varieties of English Rose the petals towards the center fail to open normally and become folded, while the outer petals open completely. This type of flower is described as being "quartered." In another type, the small petals at the center of the flower remain folded in the shape of a button, hence the term "button-eye." Flowers may be sculptured into various forms, opening either flat or with a slight turn-up at the edges to give us a shallow cup. Alternatively, the petals may turn down at the edges to form a dome.

In a large-petaled variety the flowers may form a round "cup" or "chalice." When there are no inner petals, so that the stamens within are visible, it is an "open cup." The more usual form is when it is filled with numerous small petals. A "full cup" is when the cup is brimming with petals. When the petals

Massed plantings of English Roses present a dramatic array of beautiful flower shapes, their delicious scents wafting across this small entrance garden.

FLOWER FORMS

The illustrations here show some of the commonest forms of flower to be found among the Old and English Roses. Variations on each type are often encountered.

"incurve" to form a ball or globe, we refer to the shape of the flower as "globular." If, instead of incurving, the petals turn down, we have a "deeply domed" flower.

There are, among the English Roses, varieties with "single" and "semi-double" flowers. By normal criteria there would be no reason to describe these as "English Roses," since they do not have the "Old Rose" flower, but where the overall character of a plant seems in keeping with the group as a whole, they can be included with English Roses. Certainly single blooms, with their elegant stamens, can be very beautiful.

Between these various forms there are all kinds of gradations. No two varieties will have exactly the same form of flower and the petals can play all manner of tricks, giving numerous beautiful and interesting effects. The situation is further complicated by the flower constantly changing with age. It may begin as a very definite "cup," and end its life as a "rosette." The terminology we give to the various flower shapes, however, always refers to the final form.

An effective grouping of 'Gertrude Jekyll;' its dainty, pink buds develop in stages into the true Old Rose formation of the fully open bloom.

The English Roses extend the color range of Old Rose-type flowers into the yellow spectrum. 'The Pilgrim' is a characteristically soft shade, fading to white at the edges of the blooms.

Color and Texture

Color is one of the most important attributes of the flower. It is closely associated with the texture of the petals, which both reflect and absorb light. The recent history of the rose has been marked by the development of new and ever-brighter colors, in particular strong yellows, brilliant reds and vermilions, as well as a vast range of colors both outside and within this spectrum. These colors are not necessarily bad in themselves, but I think that they are often unsuitable for roses. There is certainly a place for a splash of brilliant red in a garden consisting largely of pastel shades, but on the whole the rose is a flower that looks better in softer and richer colors. Every flower has its own best colors; those which are suitable for an iris are not necessarily so for a rose. Moreover, as in the fabrics and paints that we use in our everyday lives, there are good, bad and distinctly nasty colors, as well as poor mixtures of colors.

Breeders of Hybrid Teas and Floribundas are beginning to come round to this view, and many of their new varieties are appearing in shades that are considerably less harsh than before. In 1986 a Dutch nurseryman who grows English Roses for distribution throughout Europe reported that the demand for roses there was two-thirds for bright red and one-third for all other colors – which gave us little hope for our roses.

Five years on, the position was exactly reversed. The English Roses at present come largely in the more delicate shades of pink, apricot, peach, lilac, yellow and cream, with a few crimson, purple and mauve varieties. In addition, we look for colors which are pure and without taint of others. There was a time when clear, pure pinks with no yellow undertones were only to be obtained from among the Old Roses. This clarity, or purity, of color has been inherited by the English Roses and we would like to keep it that way. Many modern varieties are so mixed in color from generations of cross-breeding that it is very difficult to find an unalloyed shade among them.

One of the great advantages of the "Old Rose" shape of flower is that the numerous, often closely packed petals produce a depth of subtle tints. This is due not only to the number of petals, but also to the reflection of the light between and through them. Rose petals can vary widely – sometimes silky or sheeny, sometimes almost transparent. It is probably the ever-changing reflection of light in them that above all gives the English Roses their unique charm and glowing color.

GROWTH AND FOLIAGE

The growth of the plant is scarcely less important than the flower itself. It is, of course, true that the individual bloom of a rose is a thing of beauty and even if we had no more than this, the rose would still be worth cultivating. In the latter half of the nineteenth century, roses were grown almost exclusively for the individual flower and little thought was given to the habit of the plant. This was the age of the "exhibition rose" when the quality of the flower was everything. There is, however, much more to the rose than this: it is not only our best-loved flower, but also our most popular garden plant. It is important therefore that its growth should be neither ugly nor ungainly.

Most Modern Roses tend to be stiff and upright in habit – and this may indeed be a virtue in a bedding rose. An English Rose, however, is essentially a border plant and should ideally have a pleasing, natural habit of growth. This may take many forms; just as variation is desirable in the flower, so it is in the growth of the plant. English Roses range in height from the short,

Another example of the soft, muted tones of the English Roses, 'Tamora' here makes a good, low-growing partner to the yellow-centered Sisyrinchium striatum.

18in (40cm), to the tall, 7–8ft (2.5m), although mostly they fall somewhere in between (the average is around 3–4 feet/a metre). They may be narrow and upright, or broad; they may be dense, twiggy and bushy, or they may send up long arching growth to form a wide, graceful shrub. All these diverse habits add greatly to the pleasure we get from roses and to their value and use as plants for different purposes and positions in the border or garden.

Breeding for a good habit of growth is always difficult and in this respect English Roses, while always pleasing, still have room for improvement. For all their virtues, roses in general are not naturally good garden plants and a common *Berberis*, for example, may in many ways have a superior shape and form of growth, even though it may not have a fraction of the beauty of a rose. In the wild a rose is a briar, sending up powerful shoots each year to rise above and compete with neighboring plants, trees or shrubs. The breeder has taken the rose and, as best he could, controlled it by selection. The unruliness of the rose is both its charm and its weakness. It is the rose breeder's job to develop these characteristics to best advantage for the gardener; equally, it is the gardener's job to put them to best use in the garden.

Another important aspect of English Roses is the foliage, for it is this that forms the setting for the beauty of the flowers which it can do so much to enhance. One of the most satisfying periods of the rose year is the first burst of the leaf buds and the gradual formation of the fresh, young leaves, bringing with them a promise of the summer to come. The texture of leaves among English Roses can vary considerably due to the mixed origins of this group. Being basically crosses between Modern Roses, with their shiny leaves, and Old Roses, with their more opaque leaf surfaces, English Rose varieties can display either of the two extremes, as well as something in between. 'Abraham Darby,' for instance, has polished leaves that are almost like those of a Hybrid Tea Rose; in contrast, the leaves of 'The Reeve' have a dull, matt surface, more characteristic of an Old Rose. English Rose foliage can also vary greatly

Arching gracefully over the surrounding herbaceous plants are the long elegant stems of 'Lucetta;' this habit of growth can be extremely useful within a border.

The plentiful shiny leaves of 'Abraham Darby' make a perfect backdrop for its large, apricot and pink blooms. Foliage is an important part of a rose's value in a garden setting.

'The Countryman' has blooms of true Old Rose character. As it matures, it may relax its rather upright branches to form a graceful spreading bush.

in size and shape. For example, 'Claire Rose' has large, modern-type leaves, whereas 'The Countryman' has long, drooping leaves with quite small, widely spaced leaflets, as in the Damask Roses.

It is not possible – nor desirable – to say that a certain type of foliage is either "good" or "bad." I am frequently asked why our roses cannot all have foliage like that of an Old Rose, which would on the whole be my preference. However, I believe that differences between the varieties adds to the interest of the group, and anyhow it is difficult when taking certain qualities from a Modern Rose not to expect to see some influence from that rose in the foliage of its offspring. What counts is that the foliage should be suitable and plentiful, though even here we cannot be too dogmatic: even spiky, upright stems with rather sparse leaves can sometimes be attractive.

In the English Roses we are constantly endeavoring to combine beauty of flower and growth in one plant. Obviously, some varieties score more highly than others. 'Lucetta,' 'Golden Celebration' and 'Lilian Austin' are good examples of long, graceful, arching growth; 'Mary Rose,' 'Heritage,' 'Redouté' and 'Abraham Darby' have nice, bushy, shrubby growth; 'St Cecilia' has slightly arching growth, bending forward to present its flowers in an elegant and attractive way; and 'Glamis Castle,' 'Wife of Bath,' 'Country Living' and 'The Herbalist' are all short, bushy and twiggy varieties.

HEALTH AND VIGOR

As well as the esthetic qualities, we should also consider more practical matters. The plant must thrive and grow vigorously, producing its flowers as freely and regularly as possible. Health is a problem with most garden roses. It is sometimes suggested that the recent relative decline in popularity of the Hybrid Tea and Floribunda Roses has to do with the need to spray them against diseases and pests, which takes time and considerable trouble throughout the growing season. (My own view is that the decline is more due to the public becoming bored with the over-exposure of a limited range of varieties.) Whatever the case, health is now a factor that we take very seriously in all aspects of our rose breeding.

All recent varieties of English Roses sent out from our nurseries have had eight years of tests to assess their resistance to disease. There are as yet no completely disease-free garden roses – and this applies to the English Roses as much as to other classes – although certain wild species may be free of disease. As the years go by, we gain increasing experience in this field and have hopes of eventually achieving a high degree of resistance. If we were willing to sacrifice – which we are not – the beauty of the flower and the growth, we could achieve health in our roses more easily. It is, however, a matter of balancing the two; where there have been

'Gruss an Aachen' is a strongly growing English Rose, whose pearly pink flowers here add charm to a mixed border of English and Shrub Roses. The Rambler behind is 'Goldfinch.'

considerable advances made in disease-resistance it has, in my view, often been gained at the expense of the beauty of the flower.

Vigor and the ability to thrive under what are not always ideal conditions are also vital factors in our breeding of roses. Here we have made big advances since the early days; some might even feel that we have over-compensated in recent years to make up for the weakness in some of the early varieties.

Since repeat-flowering is generally not a natural phenomenon in roses (only the Species Roses *R. rugosa*, *R. fedtschenkoana* and *R. bracteata* are repeat-flowering in the wild), man's quest for this quality has placed a great strain on them. This is why it has never been easy to breed good recurrent-flowering roses and why successful new varieties are so highly prized. Strength has to be bred in, often by the introduction of new blood from strong-growing Species Roses. With the English Roses, the task has perhaps been even more difficult, as we require our roses to be more than just bedding roses – to be naturally growing shrubs. Whereas the Hybrid Tea and Floribundas are pruned almost to the ground each season, English Roses have to be able to sustain larger growth while at the same time pushing up regular flushes of bloom.

For this reason it is probably true to say that on the whole the English Roses repeat a little less regularly than other Modern Roses. Their tendency is to provide two good displays of blooms early in the season: the first from the side-shoots of the previous year's growth and the second from strong shoots at the base of the plant. Then there is something of a lull, with only occasional new blooms until late in the season when there will be another large flush. Some varieties are more continuous than this, 'Mary Rose' and its two sports, 'Winchester Cathedral' and 'Redouté,' 'Glamis Castle' and 'L.D. Braithwaite' being good examples. Continuity of flower will vary according to the climate in which a rose is growing. In a warm climate, such as California's, there will be two large crops, one in the spring and a second in the autumn. In a northerly climate, where the growing season is short, as for example in Scotland, it may be difficult to get the last crop in before the winter arrives. Early pruning will lengthen the season.

One of the most continuous-flowering of the crimson English Roses, 'L.D. Braithwaite' has richly colored blooms that look particularly fine here against purple Nepeta.

A riot of English Roses, with the contrasting spires of foxgloves, bring their own special character to this garden set amidst breathtaking mountain scenery.

CHARACTER

The ideal English Rose should have, over and above all the other characteristics already mentioned, one further quality – that is, "appeal" or "character." This notion is extremely difficult to put into words, but is nonetheless one to which I return repeatedly. It is more than just a sum of the various parts: beauty, strength, health, repeat-flowering, fragrance and so on. It is an intrinsic quality which is immediately recognizable in the feel and look of an Old Rose and is usually absent in the Modern Roses. This "old-world" character is best summed up in a triumvirate of virtues – softness, delicacy and prettiness. These elusive qualities, which belong more to the rose than to any other garden plant, are what we are trying to emphasize in the breeding of English Roses. All our English Roses have been bred with a view to achieving this; those found to be lacking are discarded. Such qualities are easily lost through insufficiently careful selection.

One or two other breeders are, I am pleased to see, taking up English Roses, and I am anxious that they should not lose the elusive character of the English Rose in the varieties that they breed. How such an identity can be maintained in a class of roses is difficult to say, since it is almost impossible to lay down the sort of rules that we find in International Rose Trials. Whereas there is little difficulty about legislating for such practical matters as health, vigor and freedom of flower, it is much harder to impose standards for the more intangible esthetic qualities. Yet I consider it vital to improve and maintain these standards and to ensure that the concept of an English Rose is properly appreciated and understood.

THE FRAGRANCE OF THE ENGLISH ROSE

Fragrance, it has been said, is the "soul" of the rose. This may be a little high-flown, but the idea is perhaps not so far-fetched as it might seem. Like the soul, fragrance is difficult to pin down because it has no substance. It is not something we can hold in our hands – it is always shifting and changing.

The sense of smell is the most subjective of the human senses. Whereas no one knows exactly how another person sees, we can at least define and measure sight. Colors are hard to put into words too, but we are all at least agreed on a set of values and associations which give them meaning. When it comes to scent, we have no such aids and are generally at a loss as to how to describe the multitude of different fragrances we encounter. Even the extent to which we are sensitive to smells varies from one individual to another, and certainly few of us are used to translating our sensations into language which can communicate the idea to others. The closest association is perhaps with taste, but although we have no difficulty in distinguishing between what is sweet or sour, salty or bitter to the tongue, we lack the vocabulary to identify the subtle variations in smell that the nose savors. In spite of this – or perhaps because of it – scents have great power to move us emotionally, working on some of the deepest associations in our memory.

It is the fragrance of the rose that above all has been responsible for its enduring popularity through the ages. Up to now the Old Roses have rightly claimed pre-eminence in fragrance among all the hybridized groups; the Modern Roses, including the Hybrid Teas and Floribundas, may have a greater variety of scents but they are generally less sumptuously perfumed than the old varieties. Rose scent, which is carried largely in the petals (though sometimes in the stamens) of the

'Evelyn' (opposite) and 'Gertrude Jekyll' (above, with Echium candicans*) are two of the most fragrant of all the English Roses. Both produce large blooms of the highest quality.*

flower, is emitted into the air most strongly when the growth of the flower and the atmospheric conditions are right. Double roses have, for obvious reasons, a greater volume of scent than single roses; and the best conditions are when the air is still, warm and moist, and not too dry. Scent, which is used by plants to attract insects acting as pollinators, is released when the essential oil, known as "attar," is dispersed as the flowers open. Roses have some of the most varied and complex fragrances of all garden plants and the distillation of rose essence has been a flourishing industry in many parts of the world for a number of centuries. Today rosewater, which is still believed to have curative properties, continues to be used for cosmetics and culinary purposes.

Building on this essential ingredient of the Old Roses has always been an important part of the breeding of English Roses. With very few exceptions, the varieties that we have used as foundation stock for English Roses were all very fragrant, and the roses we have since brought into their breeding are even more so. We have also been lucky, for although our early English Roses were strongly scented, they might easily not have been. As every rose breeder will know, it is quite possible to cross two very aromatic roses and get a rose that has no scent at all. Fortunately, it seems that fragrance is now so well embedded in the English Roses that most new varieties we have bred in recent years have it to a very high degree. As you approach an exhibit of English Roses at a flower show, this becomes immediately apparent, for you are met by a waft of rich fragrance – something that would not be the case with Modern Roses. Whether the roses are bred by us or by other breeders, I am very anxious that this standard is maintained. This requires great vigilance. It is tempting to introduce a really beautiful rose that we know has no scent and occasionally, but not often, this may be justified. If we then bred from such roses, however, scent could virtually disappear before we realized it. As things stand today, I think it is not an exaggeration to say that English Roses are, as a group, the most fragrant of all roses, even the Old Roses.

Until we bred 'Constance Spry,' the myrrh fragrance had not appeared in a new garden rose since the 1830s and 40s, when the Ayrshire Rambler Roses were first introduced.

Graham Stuart Thomas, in his classic three-volume work, *The Old Shrub Roses* (1955), *Shrub Roses of Today* (1962) and *Climbing Roses Old and New* (1965), identifies a great number of different rose scents. For example, in some varieties he detects the fragrance of honeysuckle; in others the scent of sweet pea, primrose, clove or fresh apple. He was, of course, considering the fragrances of the whole genus of the rose, including Ramblers and Species, but the English Roses on their own are capable of a wide repertoire of scents, due, no doubt, to the diverse roses in their breeding. No two rose bushes ever have quite the same perfume, but there are four principal categories of fragrance into which the English Roses can be classified.

"MYRRH"

Many of our earliest varieties had an almost unique, spicy fragrance sometimes described as that of myrrh. Not everyone agrees with this term, which only serves to emphasize the subjective nature of the sense of smell. Graham Thomas, however, tested some myrrh against the scent of these roses, and insists that the comparison is accurate.

Exactly how this scent occurred in our roses is something of a mystery. The only answer I can suggest is that 'Belle Isis,' one of the founding parents of the English Roses, may have had among its antecedents a variety of the Ayrshire Roses called 'Ayrshire Splendens.' Ayrshire Roses were some of the first Rambler Roses, well known for their hardiness. 'Ayrshire Splendens,' also known as the 'Myrrh-scented Rose,' is

The large, opulent flowers of 'Charmian' carry the luxurious "Old Rose" fragrance to a marked degree. The rose has strong, spreading growth, and can be trained as a short climber.

the only rose, as far as I am aware, to have this particular fragrance. The first English Rose, 'Constance Spry,' was a cross between 'Belle Isis' and 'Dainty Maid' and has this scent to a marked degree.

The myrrh fragrance has also been passed on to a number of other varieties of English Rose, such as 'Chaucer' and 'Cressida,' and has been mingled with other scents of still further varieties making possible a whole range of different fragrances.

"OLD ROSE"

As the first varieties of English Rose were again crossed with other roses, including further Old Roses such as the Portlands, Bourbons and so on, we began to get what is usually known as the "Old Rose" fragrance. This is the perfume that we associate with the original European Roses, before the arrival of the China Rose. It is a particularly luxurious scent and, of all the various rose fragrances, perhaps the most beautiful. Among the English Roses an outstanding example is 'Gertrude Jekyll,' which I regard as being one of the strongest and sweetest smelling of all roses. Other varieties notable for this fragrance include 'Charmian' and 'The Countryman,' and the crimson rose 'The Prince.'

"TEA ROSE"

Another scent which is found in the English Roses is that of the Tea Rose. This pleasingly fresh fragrance arrived with the first China Roses at the end of the eighteenth century and has descended through many generations of Hybrid Tea Roses and Noisette Roses to become one of the main English Rose fragrances. Some have described it as a very slightly "tarry" smell reminiscent of China tea leaves; while others disagree with this definition, nobody can deny that the aroma is

'Graham Thomas' is notable for its lovely "Tea Rose" fragrance. With its many other good qualities, this yellow variety is one of the best and most popular of the English Roses.

delicious. In the English Roses it is particularly prevalent in varieties of yellow coloring, such as 'Jayne Austin' and 'Graham Thomas.' 'Sweet Juliet' also carries the fragrance.

"FRUIT SCENT"

Last, and perhaps of least importance as far as the English Roses are concerned, we have what is generally known as a "fruit" fragrance – that is, a fragrance reminiscent of freshly picked apples or perhaps raspberries. This is a sharp scent, quite different from other more heady rose fragrances. Though not a favorite of mine, I would not like to be without it for it adds a further surprise to the pleasure of "sniffing" roses and detecting yet another scent. In the main, it derives originally from the Wichuraiana Hybrids, the class to which the majority of Rambler Roses belong. From them it descended to a number of Modern Climbing Roses which have been used in the breeding of such English Roses as 'Leander' and 'Yellow Button.'

THE COMPLEXITY OF FRAGRANCE

Although I have categorized the four main fragrances of the English Roses, I must not give the impression that they can be placed in neat slots, for this is far from true. In fact, English Roses are of such mixed origin and so intermingled in their breeding that all sorts of gradations of scent can be identified. Much of the interest and pleasure we derive from smelling the roses at close range could be heightened if we were to educate our sense of smell to make distinctions, much as we do the palette to detect the subtleties and blends of taste in foods.

In 1991 we introduced a rose called 'Evelyn' for Mr Cyrus Harvey, the proprietor of the well-known firm of perfumers, Crabtree & Evelyn. It was his idea to produce a range of products bearing the 'Evelyn' rose fragrance – something which had never been done before with any individual variety of rose. This rose is not only one of the finest we have bred, but also in our view possibly even surpasses 'Gertrude Jekyll' as the most fragrant – if one can ever be sure of such matters. In collaborating on this interesting project with Crabtree & Evelyn we were able to improve our somewhat scanty knowledge of the chemistry of a rose's fragrance. We were astonished to learn, for example, that, according to the analysis performed by a French expert for the perfume industry, the 'Evelyn' rose essence contained no fewer than 84 different chemicals – and these included acetone and benzine. Even if we can assume that by no means all of these have an effect on its fragrance, it does illustrate very clearly the bewildering complexity of nature – and of fragrance in particular.

Since scent is one of the most important attributes of the rose, I would like to see the day when roses could be chosen not only for color, shape and growth, but also for fragrance. I mean not only the strength of fragrance, but also its distinctive character. We would then choose not just a pink or a yellow rose, of a certain size and height, but a rose of a particular scent – perhaps fruity or spicy, or some other quality that appeals to us. This, I am sure, would add greatly to the pleasure of owning a collection of roses. Planting roses for their association of fragrances could then be given as much care as we give to mixing plants for their textures, colors, foliage or form. It would also surely be a help if we could invent a language for fragrance so that books and catalogues could convey to the gardener a rose's special fragrance with some degree of accuracy.

We have put considerable effort not only into breeding as much fragrance as possible into the English Roses, but also into developing a better and wider range of scents. For it is a fact that, whereas nearly all rose perfumes are pleasing, some are more pleasing than others and just occasionally we come across a rose in our hybridization program that has a positively unpleasant scent; when this happens, the rose is of course immediately discarded. For the most part, I believe we have recaptured in the English Roses many of the rose scents of the past, and in certain cases extended the repertoire of rose fragrances.

The English Roses are so fragrant that an arrangement can scent a whole room. This one includes 'Bibi Maizoon,' 'The Nun,' 'Lucetta,' 'Peach Blossom' and 'Glamis Castle.'

English Roses in the Garden

One of the many virtues of the English Roses is their compatibility, like that of the Old Roses, with other garden plants. English Roses offer us the choice of growing them in a mixed border, planting them in association with Old Shrub Roses or even grouping them in beds on their own. They can be relied upon to take their place in the garden, giving a wonderful effect throughout the summer.

From the middle of the nineteenth century, with the arrival of the Hybrid Perpetuals and towards the end of the century the Hybrid Teas, the rose began to lose much of its traditional value as a garden flower – a setback from which it is only recently beginning to recover. There were a number of reasons for this phenomenon. The first was the vogue for the exhibition rose, which meant that breeders concentrated on breeding roses almost entirely for the show bench, focusing on the individual blooms to the exclusion of all other qualities.

In the first part of this century there was another development that contributed to the decline of the rose as a garden plant. As the Hybrid Teas, and later the Floribundas, grew rapidly in popularity, so the fashion for the rose as a bedding plant took hold. The low, even growth and extended period of flowering of these roses meant that they were admirably suited to being grown in formal beds dedicated to them alone. Unfortunately, it was these very qualities, together with their often strident colors, that made them so unsuitable for use in the border or in the garden as a whole. Here a more graceful, bushy, natural habit of growth and a more amenable palette of colors are called for.

Spiky shapes always contrast well with the heavy, petal-filled flower forms of the English Roses. 'Mary Rose' is here planted with Veronica spicata *and the white* Aconitum napellus *'Albidum.'*

The repeat-flowering characteristics of these roses – which made them such good bedding roses – also diminished, paradoxically, the overall role of the rose in the garden. Repeat-flowering is closely linked with short growth; in these roses the plant does not waste its energy on building up into a large shrub, but continually produces flower shoots from the base of the bush. There is no reason why a repeat-flowering rose should not also be a good garden shrub, but there is no doubt that extended flowering is much more difficult to achieve in a Shrub Rose than in a bedding rose. A Shrub Rose expends its energy on sustaining growth rather than on producing flowers.

With the English Roses it has been our specific aim to breed roses that can provide both beauty of the individual flower – a perfect bloom is, after all, one of the great joys of the summer – and a pleasing, shrubby

A path bisects two mixed borders of roses and herbaceous plants, with box as edging. Roses will give of their best if they do not have to compete for space and nutrients.

habit of growth that makes for a good garden plant. Many other Modern Shrub Roses are repeat-flowering, and some are excellent plants. But almost all tend towards the Modern Roses in character and rarely have very well developed flowers. The great appeal of the English Roses lies in the individual flower; at the same time they are fine shrubs that can be incorporated into all kinds of creative plantings. Sharing with the Old Roses their soft colors and natural habit of growth, they make eminently sympathetic companions to other plants in a mixed border as well as to each other. Whereas previously one may have opted for an Old Rose and chosen companions to compensate for its long season out of flower, now it is possible to choose an English Rose and build color schemes for the whole summer around their beautiful blooms.

PRACTICAL CONSIDERATIONS

There are many ways to use English Roses in a garden. Before covering them in any detail, however, there are two practical points that I consider to be of paramount importance for any successful planting scheme using English Roses, or indeed any repeat-flowering rose. The first consideration is the matter of planting in groups, and the second is that of avoiding competition from neighboring plants. We have to remember that the ability to flower more than once in a season does not come naturally to a rose: this is a characteristic that has been gradually bred into it by man. The production of so many flowers over such a long period, as well as the fact that these are generally double with many more petals than the original rose species possessed, puts considerable strain upon the plant. It is unreasonable to expect that any such rose will make a large, full shrub of the density that we find in a once-flowering Old Rose, or that it will be able to withstand close competition. This problem is not of course unique to English Roses and applies just as much to certain repeat-flowering China, Bourbon and Portland Roses as well as to Hybrid Teas and Floribundas.

The first solution is to plant, wherever possible, in close groups of perhaps two, three or more plants of a single variety (see page 147). They should be positioned about 18in (50cm) apart within the group, a little wider for larger-growing varieties. In this way they will grow together to form what is, to all intents and purposes, a single shrub – with two or three points of access to the soil. Such a shrub, or shrubs, will be much more shapely and dense than when roses are individually planted, and will give a much larger and more continuous display of flowers. In small gardens, where everything is on a reduced scale, planting singly is, of course, completely justified, although even here two or more compact roses planted together will produce a stronger effect.

There is nothing particularly original in recommending group planting. With herbaceous plants and small shrubs it is an accepted practice, although it is still underused, in my view, for Shrub Roses. English Roses, and indeed any plant, will benefit from being grown in clumps and not just dotted about haphazardly in a border: a single English Rose can easily become lost amid the abundant growth of neighboring plants. Group planting may be more expensive to begin with, but in the long term the results will easily justify the additional cost: not only will you have avoided the "bitty" effect of single planting, but also you will have been able to make a more powerful impact and a much more definite statement with concentrated groups of the same plant.

The second consideration is to choose with great care the plants to place around your roses. Just as repeat-flowering qualifies a rose's potential for forming a dense shrub, so it also reduces its ability to withstand competition. This is true of English Roses and for the majority of other repeat-flowering roses. These roses should always be allowed the upper hand – even when they are planted alongside less robust herbaceous plants, they must be allowed ample space. This will not only let the roses compete to greater effect, but also provide enough room for the fertilizing and other special attention that they require. Obviously, the gap should not be so large as to upset the general line and flow of the border as a whole. It is worth mentioning here that when any kind of rose is planted with other plants, you should give it the same cultural attention that you would if it were in a border exclusively of roses; it is easy to forget this in the rough and tumble of the mixed border.

PLANNING AHEAD

As with all forms of gardening, it is important to plan ahead before planting. By looking at the rose portraits and reading the descriptions of the various varieties (pages 79–143), you will be able to visualize the size, character and color of the rose as a mature shrub. This will then allow you to imagine where your roses might best be placed, and to decide which plants should be chosen to accompany them. English Roses are, as I have mentioned before, at ease with a great variety of other shrubs and particularly with herbaceous plants. Their long flowering season ensures that they will be in flower before many of their neighboring plants and will

Several plants of 'Cymbeline' have here been planted together to form one glorious mass – demonstrating the advantages of group planting, where space allows.

Careful orchestration of heights and plant shapes will produce the most harmonious border. Here 'Graham Thomas' grows with Gentiana lutea, Delphinium *'Black Knight' and* Aconitum napellus.

continue when most of them have finished. In a mixed border they will provide that sense of permanence that all shrubs have: when the perennials have disappeared below ground for the winter, they will still be there.

English Roses can be treated in much the same way as Old Roses, except that their extended flowering means that you may have to think more carefully about the colors of surrounding plants. There is no set of rules to which you must adhere, and the possibilities for pursuing your own ideas in the garden are infinite. One of the pleasures of gardening is the element of chance – many of the happiest associations of plants are in fact the result of accident. When this happens you should build upon it; and those combinations that fail to please can always be removed or changed.

ENGLISH ROSES IN THE MIXED BORDER

For most of us, the rose is the most important and best loved flower in the garden. However, for reasons of space, it usually has to find its place alongside other plants, rather than being given a whole border to itself. Here the English Roses are much more accommodating than most other Modern Roses, whose often harsh colors and hard lines make them unsuitable companions in mixed borders. With Hybrid Teas and Floribundas, we can have conflicts, which is why we are often advised to plant them in beds of a single variety. Perhaps the worst mistake that one can make with the English Roses is to treat them as just another Modern Rose. When planted in the same border as Hybrid Teas and Floribundas the particular beauty of the English Roses is all but destroyed: the two just do not mix.

The form and structure of a mixed border needs careful thought. It is important, for example, to consider the height of a rose variety to be planted and to make sure that it is in proportion to the plants around it. On the whole, tall, very upright roses, such as 'Financial Times Centenary,' 'Charles Austin' and 'Swan' would be best at the back of the border, where their long, not very leafy growth could be masked by shorter, more bushy plants in front of them. But try to avoid a too level appearance in your border: it is all too easy to end up with a football stadium effect, with plants stacked neatly according to their height. A gentle undulation, with clumps of different heights, would be ideal, and an occasional tall variety standing out from the rest may enliven the overall effect.

Several varieties of English Rose can be trained as short climbers up, for example, trelliswork pyramids, an effective way to give a border height. The rose to the left is 'Rosy Cushion.'

This pleasingly graduated border contains 'Windrush,' an excellent Shrub Rose although one I no longer classify as an English Rose, with 'Wife of Bath' behind.

Careful choice of varieties is important here. Some, for example, 'Lucetta,' 'Cymbeline,' 'Dove,' 'English Elegance,' 'Lilian Austin,' 'Bibi Maizoon,' 'The Reeve' and 'Warwick Castle,' have particularly arching growth which forms an excellent contrast to plants with other habits. Varieties like 'Mary Rose,' 'Heritage,' 'Abraham Darby,' 'Jayne Austin,' 'Perdita' and 'Graham Thomas' have more rounded growth of about 4ft (1.2m) in height and can be the central focus of a planting scheme. Many English Roses have short, twiggy, bushy growth that is ideal for a position towards the front of a border. These include 'Wife of Bath,' 'L.D. Braithwaite,' 'Charles Rennie Mackintosh,' 'Glamis Castle,' 'Cottage Rose,' 'Country Living,' 'St Cecilia' and 'Peach Blossom.'

We should not depend only upon the natural habit of the rose, however: a little artifice can be helpful. When pruning, do not make the common mistake of removing all the growth of a rose regardless of the effect that this might be making. Sometimes horizontal or other branches can be left to retain the broad character of a bush (for further details on pruning see pages 146–9). The branches of 'The Countryman,' for example, have a habit of growing upright at first and later flopping down. It will make a much more satisfactory shrub if the branches can be held down towards the soil by means of pegging (see page 147), to leave a broad, spreading plant that will branch upwards, filling out the bush. 'The Reeve,' 'Bibi Maizoon,' 'Hero' and others would respond well to similar treatment, depending on where and how you choose to grow them.

PLANT ASSOCIATIONS

Much of the pleasure of gardening is to be had in mulling over planting associations, and the most I can hope to do here is to hint at some that the gardener might try with English Roses. In a climate other than that of Britain, gardeners will, out of cultural necessity, have to come up with their own answers. I cannot do

The frothing forms of many common herbaceous plants and herbs, such as Geranium psilostemon *and* Nepeta *Six Hills Giant, always make good partners to the heavy flowers of Old and English Roses.*

Palm trees make a suitably extravagant backdrop for the sumptuous blooms of 'Gertrude Jekyll.' Few contrasts of form or foliage could be as dramatic as this.

justice to the full scope of possibilities, and there is much to be said for leaving the choice to the gardener. I can, however, give some general pointers for the English Roses in the mixed border and indicate some of my own preferences for companion plants, most of which are hardy in Zones 4–9.

Personally I find the English Roses are more at home with herbaceous plants than with shrubs, although I find it hard to say exactly why. Perhaps it is because herbaceous perennials are very much garden plants, whereas many shrubs seem half creatures of the wild: the more sophisticated English Roses seem almost out of place in their company. Whatever the reason, my favorite choice of partners for roses would be herbaceous plants. Once again, it is essential to bear in mind that repeat-flowering roses should never have to compete with other plants.

It is a good idea to look for plants that either contrast with or complement the form and rounded blooms of the rose. English Roses often look their best when seen jutting out from the lower growth of other subjects. For plants with relatively low and airy growth you could choose aquilegias, *Stachys byzantina* (*S. lanata*), perennial scabiosa, low hardy geraniums, rosemary, or *Helichrysum italicum* (*H. angustifolium*). The light, feathery flowers of plants such as *Alchemilla mollis*, gypsophila, *Thalictrum speciosissimum* and *Crambe cordifolia* set off the heavier and more "blobby" growth and flowers of the roses, but remember what I have said about competition. In the opposite direction, effective contrast can also be achieved with the broad, sculptured leaves of hostas and bergenias. As an alternative, you might think of echoing the rose shapes with similar flower forms, such as peonies, poppies, or *Allium giganteum* with its huge globes of starry flowers.

Slender, tall, spiky plants rising out of a border that is predominantly of English Roses provide a pleasing effect. White lilies, particularly the beautiful Madonna type (*Lilium candidum*), are entirely at home, and verbascums and foxgloves, which often seed themselves wild and may have to be controlled, have their uses. Irises are good companions, especially since they flower before the roses, ensuring continuity, and afterwards their pointed foliage can provide useful contrast if the dead outer leaves are occasionally

Spiky and spire-like plants make good bedfellows for English Roses. Above, Crocosmia *flanks 'The Pilgrim,' opposite, delphiniums contribute a soft blue contrast to 'Mary Rose.'*

removed. Of course, some of the best partners for English Roses are other roses: examples of some groupings are shown on page 63.

For the "old world" charm of a typical cottage garden, you could try mixing violas, pinks, peonies, primroses and other such plants in a border with the English Roses. They will flower both before and during the roses' flowering season. Small, late-flowering bulbs, such as small narcissi and others, are all ideal, except that they may not relish the treatment given to roses later and with some their dying growth lingers on while the roses are flowering. All associations of plants, however, involve some degree of compromise and there is usually a sensible middle way to be taken.

COLOR ASSOCIATIONS

As a general rule, colors which combine well with the Old Roses also suit the English Roses. Often harmonizing partnerships work best: pinks with soft mauves and soft yellows, lilacs with creams and whites, and so on. But contrasting companions can also enliven plantings, adding dash and spirit and enriching the colors of the roses. The silver leaves of plants such as stachys, santolinas and artemisias always provide excellent background for roses of all shades, as do the glaucous gray leaves of *Ruta graveolens* and lavender in all its many forms.

For me, pink is the essential color of roses, and all other shades are subsidiary to it. The clear or blush pink shades of many English Roses – 'Gertrude Jekyll,' Kathryn Morley,' 'Heritage' are some such examples – can provide the basis of a classic English border. Neighboring flowers of deeper pink, blue, purple and mauve offer the perfect foil. English Rose varieties of a lilac or lilac-pink shade, such as 'Charles Rennie Mackintosh' and indeed 'Lilac Rose,' can be used with a similar palette of color and are valuable for putting between flowers of shades that might otherwise clash. Blues are some of the most satisfactory partnerships with pink roses; you might consider *Campanula carpatica*, or one of the many varieties in the hardy geranium family: *Geranium* 'Johnson's Blue' is one of the best, with its easy, reliable nature and summer flowers of light blue. Lavender is a favorite companion to roses, or a froth of catmint, *Nepeta* × *faassenii*, would be a possibility. Another plant that deserves a

A color partnership of soft pink – 'Kathryn Morley' – with the deep indigo tones of Geranium × magnificum. *The cranesbills are first class companion plants.*

mention is *Ceanothus* (grown on the West Coast): in mild or sheltered gardens it can create a delightful backdrop to the English Roses.

Plants with purple foliage might also be considered to partner pink roses. Low-growing choices could be the blue-flowered, purple-leaved *Ajuga reptans* 'Atropurpurea,' or the dark purple-red leaved *Heuchera* 'Palace Purple.' A good choice for a taller shrub would be *Cotinus coggygria*, since its richly colored translucent leaves would complement a pink bloom; it is worth trying to site this plant with light shining through from behind it. *Cosmos atrosanguineus* (mostly grown as an annual) is a plant worth considering: its velvety maroon flowers would complement pink blossoms, and it has an elusive, but distinctive chocolate scent. At Powis Castle the purple-flushed *Tellima grandiflora rubra* forms companion planting to the pink rose 'Chaucer;' other plants around include the gray-leaved *Anthemis sancti-johannis*, the fleshy leaves of bergenia, *Allium karataviense* and clumps of the glaucous-leaved grass, *Festuca glauca*. Such a planting demonstrates the range of possibilities.

There is no shortage of white, or whitish, plants to partner pink roses – or indeed roses of any hue. White lilies have already been mentioned; other suggestions might include the early *Phlox* 'Miss Lingard,' *Campanula persicifolia* 'Alba,' the choicer white violas, *Cistus hybridicus*, with its pink-tinged buds (Zones 8–10), and the silvery leaves of *Lamium maculatum* 'Beacon Silver' – all would provide plenty of interest once the roses' first flush of flowers was over.

The delphinium, one of the most beautiful herbaceous plants and a favorite mainstay in the English garden, would combine perfectly with the soft pastel shades of the English Roses. In their traditional colors of blue, purple and white, and with their statuesque height and spiky flowers, they would contrast well with tumbling pink roses surrounding them. *Delphinium × belladonna* 'Wendy' is a good shade, as is 'Blue Nile,' mid-blue with a white eye.

Yellow is usually a difficult color to accommodate in roses. Absent in the Old Roses, it has often appeared in Modern Roses in harsh and garish tones that can jar with other colors in a border. Yellow English Roses, on the other hand, tend to be softer in color, opening up wider possibilities for interesting associations with a number of plants in this spectrum. Many of the stronger yellow varieties, such as 'Graham Thomas' and 'Golden Celebration,' can find their place in the border, particularly if they are graduated through the apricot, peach, salmon-pink and cream range.

English Roses even in contrasting colors will mix happily. Here the yellow 'English Garden' and the pink 'Charmian' together pick out the same colors in honeysuckle.

In association with the yellow and apricot or peach English Roses there are a number of possible plants. You might try, for instance, the West Coast native *Limnanthes douglasii*, under a rose such as 'The Pilgrim' with its near-white outer petals. If you wanted more of a contrast, there are plenty of plants with bronze foliage, such as the bronze fennel, *Foeniculum vulgare* 'Purpureum,' that would partner a rose such as 'Golden Celebration.' *Crocosmia × crocosmiiflora* 'Solfaterre' also has useful bronze-flushed leaves, and many varieties of *Hemerocallis* suggest themselves for their rich orange and coppery accents. For a crisper contrast, you could choose a blue-flowered plant, such as *Salvia* × *superba* with its forest of blue spikes, delphiniums again, or one of the soft blue penstemons. Shrubs to accompany yellow roses might include *Elaeagnus pungens* 'Maculata,' its glossy leaves distinguished by a broad, bright yellow patch, *Lonicera nitida* 'Baggesen's Gold' and *Euonymus fortunei* 'Emerald 'n' Gold;' there are also a number of golden forms of hollies and ivies that would blend well with these colors.

Roses in rich red can contribute dramatic splashes of color in the garden. The English Rose 'Prospero' is a lovely crimson, and an effective partner to soft pinks.

'William Shakespeare,' whose Gallica-like, deep red blooms fade to attractive shades of purple, makes a fitting foreground to the ruins of Sudeley Castle.

Red and deep crimson roses can also sometimes be a problem and need a little extra care in their positioning. They look best next to purples and mauves, and are effective besides stronger pinks. 'L.D. Braithwaite' and 'The Prince,' among other red and crimson English Roses, can add a welcome splash of color in any border. Interspersed with plants of softer shades of pink, they can jolt an otherwise muted or pallid border into life. 'L.D. Braithwaite' is particularly useful in this respect, and like 'The Prince,' 'The Dark Lady' and most crimson English Roses to date, its flowers develop into a lovely rich purple which is most effective in conjunction with other colors.

As companions to red roses I would recommend all those listed for pink forms, with a few additions. White plants offer sharp contrast and can set off and divide the very dark red of the English Roses from flowers of pink, mauve or blue. White peonies can therefore be good, as well as white foxgloves. Soft pink flowers mingle well, and for a more arresting contrast you could choose flowers of yellow, such as *Alchemilla mollis*, *Achillea* 'Moonshine' and *Chrysanthemum frutescens* 'Jamaica Primrose.' For a climber to form a backdrop, either a honeysuckle from the yellower ranges, or the vigorous and long-flowering *Clematis orientalis*, could make an attractive partnering.

White roses can have companion plantings in the widest range of contrasting colors. In general terms, white is always useful for separating bold colors that might otherwise clash or jar. You might choose a white

English Rose to do just that. Alternatively, you might be creating an all-white garden or border. There are four white varieties of English Rose to choose from; with them you might try many of the white-flowering herbaceous perennials as well as the silver-leaved shrubs. For contrast, you could opt for a plant like the rich red *Penstemon* 'Garnet,' and use *Saxifraga* × *urbium* (London pride) to form an edging linking the two. The salmon-pink of *Geranium endressii* 'Wargrave Pink' can be difficult with the purer pink English Roses, but would blend well with either white or cream shades. A tapestry of low-growing plants, such as pansies, campanulas, catmint and veronicas, would also provide a perfect setting for white roses.

ROSE BORDERS

If you are planning a border confined to roses, you might consider one either with a mixture of Old and English Roses or of English Roses exclusively. A mixed collection will have the additional interest of a greater variety of flower, growth and leaf, with the English Roses contributing continuous blooms throughout the summer, as well as a greater range of color. The proportion of one to the other is of course a matter of personal choice. My own preference would probably be to grow mainly English Roses, with other Shrub Roses helping out. Even in an Old Rose border, however, a sprinkling of English Roses would be useful to continue the interest into the autumn. We should not, it seems to me, be too restrictive in our choice – for example, a leafy specimen of 'Roseraie de l'Haÿ' or the spreading growth of little 'White Pet' may be just what is needed in an otherwise all English Rose border to fill out a gap and complete the picture. Likewise, herbaceous plants may be added towards the edge of the border to round off an otherwise abrupt edge.

The observations I have made on the structure of the mixed border also apply here. You will have to look carefully at the habit of growth of the English Roses and decide which ones are more suitable for the back, and which for the middle or the front of the border; remember also what you can do to adapt the natural shape of a rose by careful pruning. Small groups of a single variety, carefully placed and complementing each other in form and color, will provide the most satisfactory results. Wide borders may need the help of

A glorious border of English Roses, including 'Lilian Austin.' Choosing roses with a habit of growth appropriate to their position will usually give the best effect.

A long pergola festooned with Climbing and Rambling Roses provides the backbone of the garden at our nurseries. It creates an inviting, scent-filled pathway.

something taller than the English Roses: in these cases think about adding a few Climbing Roses at the rear of the border. None of this is, I have to admit, quite as easy as it sounds, but a little shuffling at the planning stage, perhaps together with assistance from a few other plants and roses, should help you to come up with the desired result.

For those with slightly larger gardens, two parallel rose borders, divided by a path, is a worthwhile idea. The path could be of grass, brick, gravel, stone or even slabs of concrete and might lead to another part of the garden, a sitting area or to some garden ornament as a focus for the eye. It can be either straight or curved, the latter giving a more informal, flowing effect. For myself, I can think of few more pleasing experiences than to walk between two borders of Old and English Roses, their blooms billowing on to the path, their scents filling the air. Here the different varieties can be seen, compared and appreciated, and it is easy to give them the special attention that they need.

Two low-growing, informal hedges of R. gallica officinalis *make an excellent edging for a grass path. Some English Roses could fulfill the same purpose, and would repeat-flower.*

'English Garden' is one of many shorter-growing English Roses that make good bedding roses. They have the advantage over Hybrid Teas of soft colors and old-fashioned flower shapes.

Rose Beds

In Edwardian times and in the years between the wars, numerous rose gardens based on the pattern of small, formal beds of roses were constructed. This is still the most popular form of rose garden today. The ideal bedding roses are, of course, the Modern Hybrid Tea and Floribunda Roses, with their low, even growth and regular repeat-flowering. The more natural, shrubby growth of the English Roses makes them less suitable for this purpose, but there are a number of appropriate short-growing varieties. I would suggest 'Cottage Rose,' 'Glamis Castle,' 'St Cecilia,' 'The Dark Lady,' 'Ambridge Rose,' 'Evelyn,' 'Charles Rennie Mackintosh,' 'Wife of Bath,' 'Lilac Rose,' 'Tamora,' 'Bredon' and 'English Garden.' Some of these shorter varieties may grow taller in the various climate zones of North America and may not flower with quite the same continuity as a good Hybrid Tea or Floribunda, but offer the advantage of the "old" type of flower.

If you wanted to create a rose garden consisting of small island beds of roses, you would find it a little difficult to confine it to English Roses alone – the selection of varieties that are suitable is still rather limited. But there is no reason why you should not include sympathetic roses of other classes in this type of garden plan, if possible keeping one variety to a bed. Among the Hybrid Teas, you might choose 'Paul Shirville,' 'Pristine,' 'Sutter's Gold,' 'Pascali,' 'Polarstern,' and 'Mme Butterfly;' among the Floribundas, roses with similarly soft colors include 'Margaret Merril,' 'English Miss,' 'Chanelle' and 'Victoriana.' There are also some excellent Dwarf Polyanthas that would blend well with English Roses.

In large gardens and public places, Hybrid Musks and other Shrub Roses are often used to good effect in big rose beds. Some of the taller English Roses of compact nature, for example 'The Pilgrim,' 'Heritage,' 'Abraham Darby,' 'Graham Thomas,' 'Mary Rose' and 'Winchester Cathedral' might equally be used here.

In the Queen's Garden at Sudeley Castle, Gloucestershire, groupings of Old Roses are edged with sage, lavender and hyssop, and underplanted with herbs and herbaceous plants.

AN "OLD ROSE" GARDEN

Before the introduction of English Roses, a garden dedicated to Old Roses was scarcely a practicality: few gardeners would be prepared to allot so much space to Old Roses when their flowering season lasts for only a few weeks in early summer. With the chance of an extended period of bloom, however, this type of garden becomes a distinct possibility. Using either a mixture of Old Roses and English Roses or English Roses on their own, there is now exciting potential for new ways of planning an "Old Rose" garden in which the pleasingly natural character of these roses is shown to best advantage.

Plans for an "Old Rose" garden could take any number of forms, but I would like to suggest a garden layout based on a series of "rooms" with hedges, trellis or rustic work providing the "walls." The most basic kind of rose garden could consist of a single such "room" (see opposite). This need be no more than a square or oblong area, suitably enclosed, with crossing paths and some form of ornament or structural decoration to draw the eye towards a focal point at the center. Around the outside the "walls" would consist of some kind of support for Climbing Roses, thus providing the height. Taller, more rampant roses, which are almost impossible to accommodate in small rose beds, would be most effective if planted towards the rear and the roses graduated down to small varieties against the paths.

With the addition of further "rooms," linked by narrow paths crossing each other, it is not difficult to imagine how more complex arrangements could be built up. Enclosed gardens such as these suggest an atmosphere of intimacy that is particularly appropriate for English Roses; moreover, they are able to trap the fragrant scents of the blooms. Walls are best of all, and look marvelous clothed in Climbing Roses and Ramblers, but, unless your garden already has them, this may not be feasible. Dense evergreen hedges provide excellent enclosure, their dark foliage a perfect background for the lighter, more airy growth and the soft colors of the roses. It is important to make sure that any surround should not be so tall as to exclude the sunlight from the garden – a height of 6ft (1.8m) would be best. With rustic or trellis work, which would also

A GARDEN OF ENGLISH ROSES

This simple design shows how the many varieties of English Rose can be put together in beautiful color harmonies, with Climbers and Ramblers to provide height. The English Roses are planted in groups of three to five, with single plants of the vigorous 'Constance Spry' and 'Chianti' at each corner. The low-growing roses in the center should be planted in groups of perhaps eight, and pruned as bedding roses.

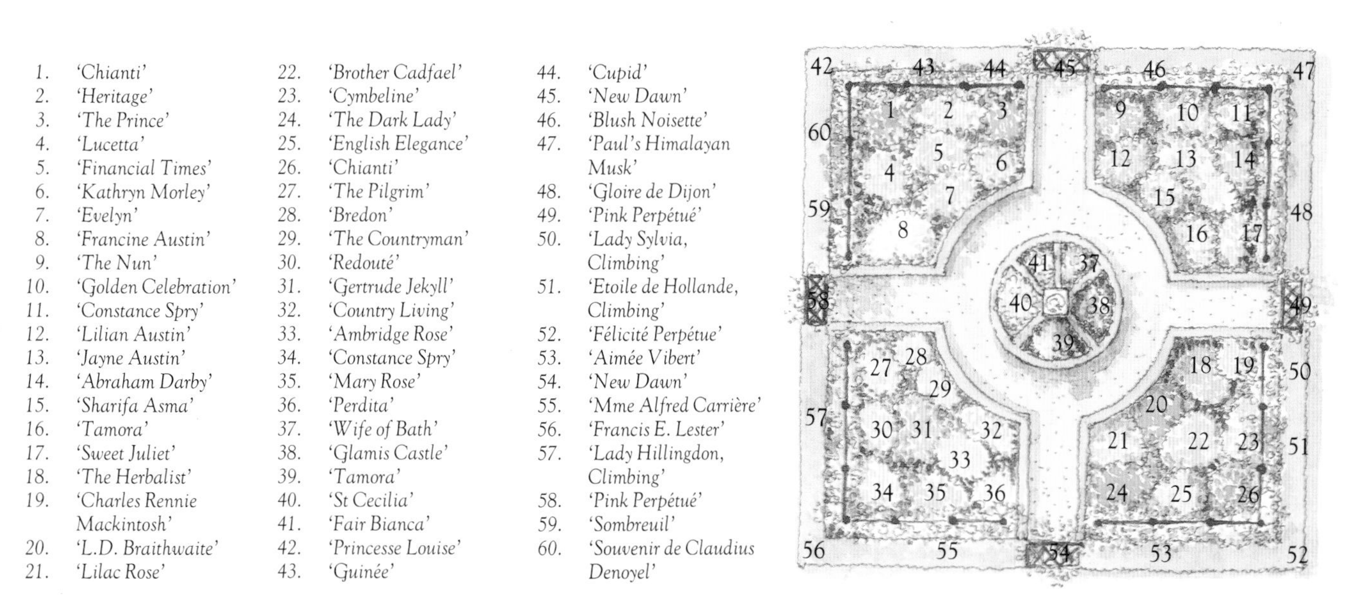

1. *'Chianti'*
2. *'Heritage'*
3. *'The Prince'*
4. *'Lucetta'*
5. *'Financial Times'*
6. *'Kathryn Morley'*
7. *'Evelyn'*
8. *'Francine Austin'*
9. *'The Nun'*
10. *'Golden Celebration'*
11. *'Constance Spry'*
12. *'Lilian Austin'*
13. *'Jayne Austin'*
14. *'Abraham Darby'*
15. *'Sharifa Asma'*
16. *'Tamora'*
17. *'Sweet Juliet'*
18. *'The Herbalist'*
19. *'Charles Rennie Mackintosh'*
20. *'L.D. Braithwaite'*
21. *'Lilac Rose'*
22. *'Brother Cadfael'*
23. *'Cymbeline'*
24. *'The Dark Lady'*
25. *'English Elegance'*
26. *'Chianti'*
27. *'The Pilgrim'*
28. *'Bredon'*
29. *'The Countryman'*
30. *'Redouté'*
31. *'Gertrude Jekyll'*
32. *'Country Living'*
33. *'Ambridge Rose'*
34. *'Constance Spry'*
35. *'Mary Rose'*
36. *'Perdita'*
37. *'Wife of Bath'*
38. *'Glamis Castle'*
39. *'Tamora'*
40. *'St Cecilia'*
41. *'Fair Bianca'*
42. *'Princesse Louise'*
43. *'Guinée'*
44. *'Cupid'*
45. *'New Dawn'*
46. *'Blush Noisette'*
47. *'Paul's Himalayan Musk'*
48. *'Gloire de Dijon'*
49. *'Pink Perpétué'*
50. *'Lady Sylvia, Climbing'*
51. *'Etoile de Hollande, Climbing'*
52. *'Félicité Perpétue'*
53. *'Aimée Vibert'*
54. *'New Dawn'*
55. *'Mme Alfred Carrière'*
56. *'Francis E. Lester'*
57. *'Lady Hillingdon, Climbing'*
58. *'Pink Perpétué'*
59. *'Sombreuil'*
60. *'Souvenir de Claudius Denoyel'*

In some settings, heavy-headed roses would be inappropriate: the fragile petals of 'Windrush,' seen in the foreground with Oenothera speciosa *'Rosea,' illustrate the charm of single and semi-double flowers.*

provide an excellent structure on which to grow Climbing Roses, the exclusion of light would be less of a problem since some would filter through.

The advantage of starting with this kind of simple plan is that it is capable of infinite expansion. Once you have laid out the first beds or borders and surrounded them with hedges or trelliswork, you can then visualize a series of such gardens, one leading into another like the rooms of a house. Rose gardens on this scale do not necessarily have to be at all extensive and even the strip-like plot stretching behind a typical town or suburban house could be transformed by dividing it up into two or three successive "rooms" to create different effects. These could be not only English Roses, but also Old Roses, perhaps with the addition of a few other plants to round out the planting scheme. Of course, such a plan could easily be incorporated into a larger, more general type of garden. The site will generally dictate the shape – and often the more difficult the site, the more interesting the garden.

In very large gardens, or parks, there can, obviously, be even greater complexities of design. Here long passageways are possible, between fairly narrow borders edged by hedges, leading the eye along vistas towards some focal end-point; sidewalks off the passageway might lead into a number of different "rooms." This is by no means a new concept in gardening – fine examples can be seen in the gardens at Hidcote Manor, Gloucestershire, and Sissinghurst Castle, Kent. In the garden at our Shropshire nurseries, we have devised a system of such interconnected "rooms," each area surrounded by hedges of Leyland cypress (yew would have been preferable, but we needed fairly instant results). We have used Climbing Roses everywhere – on wires suspended on poles behind the roses, over arches, up brick pillars connected by rustic poles and on a long pergola leading out of the garden. Short hedges of box, and in places yew, serve as edging. The intimacy that this type of layout offers is to me the best environment in which to appreciate English and Old Roses. Here we can see the individual bloom – the great glory of the rose – at close quarters, as well as enjoying the different views and angles as we turn corners to find some new surprise.

Climbing Roses and Standard Roses

Whether you are planning a mixed border with English Roses, or an "Old Rose" rose garden, height is often the dimension that is missing. This can be introduced into the garden with Climbing and Rambler Roses, which can be used either as a backdrop to a border or to delineate the contours of the garden. With the exception of 'Constance Spry,' 'Shropshire Lass' and 'Francine Austin' (which can all be persuaded to climb when planted next to a suitable support; see, for example, page 69), English Roses are not yet generally available as Climbers; for these you will have to look elsewhere. Fortunately, most Climbers and nearly all Ramblers go well with English Roses; the latter, being close to the Old Roses in type, are particularly sympathetic.

Support for Climbing and Rambling Roses can take all kinds of forms: walls (which provide protection for the more tender varieties and encourage a longer season of growth), trelliswork, arches, pergolas or simple larch poles with cross-bars (make sure that the poles have been pressure-treated to prevent decay). Some not too rampant Ramblers can occasionally be trained through

The Round Garden at our nurseries (right) is a true garden of English Roses. 'Charles Rennie Mackintosh' is in the foreground, 'Shropshire Lass' to the right, 'Francine Austin' behind.

a hedge to good effect; others can be persuaded to climb high into the branches of a tree or to clothe an old tree stump. Many of the upright varieties of roses also look charming growing up and through the elegant, free-standing metal supports sold for the purpose; these are usually no more than four metal uprights linked by braces, with a decorative twist or curve at the top. They are able to give height even when the rose is small.

Standard (Tree) Roses are also useful for creating height. The character of these roses will not suit an informal style of garden, but they have their place in a more formal setting. In a wide border of English Roses, for instance, they help to break the monotony of too level an appearance. They give an elegant touch to a rose garden, and look well flanking both sides of a path or forming the centerpiece within formal, parterre-style beds. A number of English Roses, being naturally spreading and bushy in habit, lend themselves to being grown in this way: good examples are 'Golden Celebration,' 'Bibi Maizoon,' 'Mary Rose,' 'L.D. Braithwaite,' 'Redouté,' 'The Dark Lady' and 'Glamis Castle.' What is important for Standard Roses esthetically is that they should have long stems and that these should be clearly visible, giving an overall tree-like effect. Plant Standard Roses beside shorter varieties, so that their shape is not obscured.

Weeping standards make eye-catching features, and many varieties are suitable. This fine example is 'May Queen,' growing with R. gallica *'Versicolor' (Rosa Mundi, left) and 'Charles de Mills.'*

The soft shapes of roses often benefit from a well positioned focal point. A sundial is a classic choice, seen here with the striped 'Ferdinand Pichard' on the left, 'English Garden' on the right.

GARDEN ORNAMENTS

Ornamental features in a formal rose garden can transform a rather ordinary layout into something altogether more distinguished. A rose in a large pottery urn, perhaps raised on a plinth of some kind, can provide the focal point, although sculpture would probably be my first choice. As a centerpiece or at the far end of a vista, a sculpted figure, for example, can be most effective. There are an infinite number of possibilities, however, and there is no need to spend a lot of money; there are some very good reproductions on the market and almost anything, even an *objet trouvé*, can be made into a feature to help with the structure of a garden. Before buying anything expensive it is wise to spend some time experimenting with proportions; perhaps you could temporarily place objects of various sizes to enable you to visualize how a statue might fit. A garden bench or seat can be both ornamental and useful; other alternatives you might also consider are a sundial, a fountain or a small circular pool. One or two English Roses of lax, spreading habit, such as 'Lilian Austin' or 'Bibi Maizoon,' could be planted nearby and a few branches encouraged to hang over the water so that you can see the reflection of the flowers.

ROSES IN CONTAINERS

For those with only very small gardens – or perhaps no garden at all, but just a small paved area or balcony – it may be reassuring to know that English Roses can be grown very satisfactorily in containers. All the rules of good cultivation apply equally to roses grown in pots – but more so, since these bushes will be entirely dependent on the attention you give them. Regular watering and feeding will therefore become absolutely vital (see pages 150–1).

A cottage setting for the English Rose 'Heritage,' made more dramatic by the large, rough-textured leaves of Inula magnifica *(left) and spires of* Campanula latiloba.

The following shorter or medium-sized varieties of English Rose are among the best subjects (some of the stronger varieties could even be encouraged to climb a little with the aid of support): 'Heritage,' 'Sharifa Asma,' 'Brother Cadfael,' 'Cottage Rose,' 'The Countryman,' 'The Prince,' 'The Dark Lady,' 'Golden Celebration,' 'Evelyn,' 'English Garden' and 'St Swithun.' Receptacles for roses can come in many forms – pots, urns, tubs – with the advantage that they are movable. They can adorn a small garden, sited either on their own or in matching pairs of tubs, for instance, flanking steps or a doorway. They can also provide the focus for a larger rose garden, either at the center or towards one end.

The current vogue for conservatories, many of which are sadly underused for horticultural purposes, now makes it possible for many people to grow roses under glass. Once again, feeding and watering are of prime importance, but if you can satisfy their requirements in this respect, I can promise you English Roses of unrivaled beauty. In the great days of the Victorian and Edwardian conservatories, roses were regularly grown under glass for out-of-season flowering – for cutting and arrangement in the house. Today, the magnificence of the roses at the annual Chelsea Flower Show is in some degree due to their having been grown in greenhouses – it would be impossible to have roses in bloom in Britain in late May without the aid of glass. Anyone lucky enough to have a greenhouse can achieve similarly superlative results with roses in pots, which can be taken out into the garden or brought into the house as decoration. The enthusiast will thus be rewarded with blooms of exquisite refinement, which can be appreciated at close range.

ENGLISH ROSES ELSEWHERE IN THE GARDEN

If you have ample space in your garden, you may wish to grow English Roses for their blooms alone, regardless of their role as a garden plant. This could be done for the purposes of exhibition or for cutting. You could then plant them in rows either in a bed on their own or in the kitchen garden, where, with heavy fertilizing and careful cultivation, they would be sure to produce some of the most superb blooms.

Like other Shrub Roses, English Roses can also be used as specimens in a lawn, or along a grass verge of a drive or in some similar position in the landscape. For this, choose the larger-growing varieties, planted close together in groups: 'Heritage,' 'Mary Rose,' 'Abraham Darby,' 'Graham Thomas,' 'Winchester Cathedral' and 'English Elegance' all suggest themselves. Roses such as these could be effectively ringed, as one might with a group of trees in a park, with a low fence at the height of about 3ft/1m (see page 147). As they grow and send out long branches, these could be attached to the fence and used as a basis for further branching until the

The partnership of roses and water is an unusual but very beautiful one. The pale pink 'Lucetta' features here, with other English Roses, beside a broad expanse of still water.

whole builds up to a well-supported mound. This method has been successfully implemented at Castle Howard, Yorkshire, with the once-flowering 'Constance Spry' and 'Chianti.' Other English Roses, like 'Shropshire Lass,' 'Leander,' 'Abraham Darby' and 'English Elegance,' would also be suitable for this treatment. If such groups are to stand in grass, you will need to make sure that this does not invade the growing area immediately around the roses. Regular weeding, particularly in the early years, will be essential and the turf should be edged from time to time. Once again, generous fertilizing will ensure that the roses make the vigorous growth needed for such highly prominent positions.

Like several other varieties of English Rose, 'Shropshire Lass' can be trained so that its long lax stems, decked with large, single flowers, grow up and over a support.

In this chapter I hope to have given the reader a few suggestions for the planting of English Roses; inspiration might also come from seeing how roses have been used in some of the great gardens of Britain and elsewhere. Anyone who has noticed the low hedge of *R. gallica officinalis* edging two borders at Kiftsgate Court, Gloucestershire, for example (see page 60), could easily imagine how English Roses such as 'Glamis Castle,' 'The Herbalist' or perhaps 'The Dark Lady' might be similarly adapted. It has not been practicable here to cover the full scope of possible planting schemes; each garden will offer its own innumerable opportunities.

English Roses in the Home

Few pleasures can compare with the sight – and the intoxicating scent – of a bowl of freshly picked summer roses. Whatever the skill of the flower arranger, the arrangement is always guaranteed to be a delight for all the senses; and roses will make excellent partners for a whole range of other commonly grown garden flowers that could find a place in a vase or bowl.

English Roses are among the very best subjects for flower arrangements inside the house, having not only a valuable gamut of fragrance but also the kind of informal beauty that looks as well indoors as in the garden. Hybrid Tea Roses, often thought of as the perfect cut flowers, suffer from the drawback that they are soon over – once the bud has developed into a full bloom, its shape tends to disintegrate and the individual flowers have little further decorative value. The charm of the English Roses, in contrast, is that after the bud has opened the flower continues to be beautiful, even when some of the hidden outer petals have begun to deteriorate. Tests conducted in the United States have proved that English Rose blooms generally have a longer life than those of most Modern Roses. Whereas Old Roses also look marvelous and last longer in floral decorations than most Modern Roses, their petals, being less substantial than those of the English Roses, tend to be shorter-lived.

Arrangements that reflect the natural tendencies of a rose variety work best. Left, the globe-shaped blooms of 'Bibi Maizoon' hang themselves gracefully over a vase of deep green.

With all types of roses, the first consideration is to gather the flowers from the garden in the correct fashion; a little extra care at this stage will ensure that they have a much longer life in water. If at all possible, avoid picking roses in the heat of the day, when they will have lost some of their moisture, as this will mean that they will only last for a short while when cut.

English Roses are at the height of their beauty when their flowers are completely open. Do not pick them in bud: if you do, they will fail to open properly and never make satisfactory blooms. The right time to pick them is when they are half open – they will then unfold their petals to make perfectly formed blooms.

As you gather your roses, place them immediately up to their necks in a bucket of water. When I say "immediately," I mean just that. Experiments by the cut-flower trade have confirmed that even after a few seconds out of water, the cut on the stem will start to callus over and the roses will be less able to take up water. It is worth actually cutting the end of the stem again under water after picking – thus avoiding any callusing at all. If the roses can then be left standing in

Gather roses straight into a bucket of water to ensure they last as long as possible; you will find that even the most ad hoc *arrangements look charming.*

water for a few hours, or preferably overnight, so much the better. Choose a flower with a thick stem rather than a thin, wiry one, since the former will be able to take up more water and hold it better. Cut the roses with short stems as the water has less distance to travel to reach the flowers. You will have to balance this, however, against the usefulness of longer stems as you create your flower arrangements.

THE NATURAL ARRANGEMENT

When choosing which roses to gather, you should have some idea as to where in the house you wish to place your bowl, and can therefore pick accordingly. Stiff, formal and highly stylized arrangements, beloved of flower arrangers of the recent past, are not at all suitable for English Roses and would detract from their natural beauty. The best rule is to allow the flowers themselves to dictate the size and shape of an arrangement – take your bunch of roses and simply allow it to fall loosely in the container. Having viewed the result with some care from all angles, move a flower here and there, gradually building up the shape into a pleasing overall picture. Always allow the flowers to have their own way as far as possible, rather than trying to force them into some preconceived pattern. Roses have a wilful habit of turning their heads – you can place them carefully in one position and they will immediately turn and look the other way. You will find that some blooms will have to be removed and others added, and this you can do by using the bulk of the arrangement to hold them in place. If you look critically at the extra roses as you put them in, the best position for each flower will soon become obvious: every stem will have its natural bias. Try to complement one bloom with another, perhaps on the opposite side of the bowl.

COLOR AND FORM

While the flowers themselves largely determine the form of an arrangement, the colors can be left to the choice of the flower arranger. Hybrid Teas and Floribundas, with their harsher, more metallic colors, need to be treated with caution if the result is not to be garish. English Roses, on the other hand, with their softer hues will usually blend together in perfect harmony. For example, with English Roses it is possible to combine the beautiful pink shades with the soft yellows – something you would hesitate to do with most other flowers, particularly with Modern Roses. The bright crimsons of such varieties as 'L.D. Braithwaite,' however, might need to be used with restraint if they are not to overwhelm the other colors. Some shades are particularly useful when tucked in between different colors which might otherwise not blend together well. For example, the lilac tints of 'Charles Rennie Mackintosh' and 'Lilac Rose,' the rich purple of 'The Prince' and the grayish tones of 'Cymbeline' can all have the effect of lending depth and harmony to the spectrum of neighboring colors.

To avoid an arrangement being in any way "bitty" or "blobby," it is a good idea to group various colors and

Right, airy sprays of the white, small-flowered 'Francine Austin' make a good counterpoint to heavier rose blooms in shades of pink and deep crimson.

forms together. Large- and medium-sized flowers of the English Roses can be mixed to good effect with the much smaller spray roses. The delicate, airy clusters of 'Francine Austin,' for instance, are just what is needed as a 'fill-in' between the more substantial flowers of other English Roses. Many of the Ground-cover Roses may also be used in this way, as well as the graceful Ramblers. These "fillers" should not be allowed to become too dominant – it is usually best to choose the softer shades and the lighter, more feathery flowers. The Modern Shrub Rose 'Bloomfield Abundance' is especially suitable for this purpose, having long, pointed sprays of dainty, miniature Tea Rose buds that can be encouraged to "spike" out an arrangement of English Roses.

A mixture of English Roses and Hybrid Teas and Floribundas is never a good idea. Just as this is an unsuitable alliance in the garden, so it is in the house. The "bud" formation of the Modern Roses and their often strident colors strike a discordant note when put alongside the more delicate lines and coloring of English Roses. On the other hand, Old Roses and Rambler Roses are totally compatible and can be used together with English Roses in arrangements whenever they are available.

This sumptuous arrangement of English Roses in all the strongest red and crimson shades shows the elegance of a classic, completely plain glass vase.

CHOOSING A CONTAINER

If roses are to last well in an arrangement, their stems must be placed as deeply as possible in the water. For this reason, deep containers – either small or large, round or straight-sided – are on the whole more suitable than shallow ones. You can use jugs, old teapots, buckets and all manner of other receptacles. You might even consider collecting such objects when the chance arises, the only proviso being that the container should not be of so bright a color nor so definite a design that it detracts from the flowers.

Glass vases are very flattering for roses, particularly when positioned so that the light shines through them to show the thorny flower stems. There is no need to be restricted to the use of single containers: groups can often be very effective – for example, one large bowl with one or two smaller bowls around it, or maybe a mixture of jugs, mugs and bowls.

Some of the smaller-flowered English Rose varieties placed in bowls – either alone or with other smaller, sympathetic flowers – can look charming and will show off the individual flowers to perfection. For individual blooms a long, single stem holder is ideal, especially for that one exquisite flower picked on your way back

Unusual receptacles can be charming. Here a teapot is packed with the cupped flowers of 'Bow Bells,' with sprigs of lavender, a spray of immature apples, and tiny violas.

Floating rose blooms in shallow bowls, water-lily-like, is a good way to use especially short-stemmed roses. Linking the bowls with tendrils of honeysuckle adds further charm.

from the garden. As a rose breeder, I find that a single bloom on its own is the best means of observing a promising new rose at close quarters. Wearing a rose as a buttonhole is another possibility: a small bloom of 'The Prince,' 'Fair Bianca,' 'Bow Bells' or 'Heritage' could look very handsome.

FOLIAGE

Foliage forms an essential part of any arrangement of roses. Whether you use the leaves of the English Roses themselves or those of other roses or plants, they will provide an excellent foil which will show off the blooms perfectly. Some keen flower arrangers grow roses especially for their foliage. Species Roses play a useful role here, although the dainty, light leaves of some types are more suitable for filling in between flowers than for giving a solid background. *R. glauca* (formerly *R. rubrifolia*) is probably the best of all: its purple-red stems and glaucous, coppery-mauve leaves provide an invaluable contrast for the flower arranger. Others like *R. virginiana*, with light green foliage, *R. willmottiae*, with light, fern-like foliage, and *R. villosa*, with gray-green leaves, are also worth considering. Gray-leaved plants, such as santolina, senecio, artemisia and lavender, also set off the English Roses very effectively, and the lacy, yellow-green *Alchemilla mollis* (ladies' mantle) is a first rate companion to roses in any floral decoration.

ENGLISH ROSES WITH OTHER FLOWERS

As in the garden, English Roses associate happily with many other flowers, provided that the colors and textures are sensitively chosen. On the whole, as before, the colors should not be too strong: they should complement rather than dominate the softness of the English Roses. Some combinations are particularly reliable: many of the blue flowers, for example, *Nepeta* (catmint), *Geranium* 'Johnson's Blue' and blue *Campanula* (Canterbury Bell), provide the perfect counterpart to the soft pinks, crimsons and mauves of the English Roses. Other, larger flowers to include in this color range are such herbaceous plants as peonies, delphiniums and irises. The many apricot and yellow varieties of English Rose tone well with white flowers, such as those of *Philadelphus* and *Viburnum*, and even with the strong purples of various *Salvia* and *Hebe* species. Some of the smaller "daisy" flowers, for example *Erigeron* and *Aster* × *frikartii*, also make sympathetic partners; callunas (heathers) are useful, as are the larger Michaelmas daisies later in the season.

There are almost endless variations to be played on the basic groupings of any floral composition – colors, tones, textures and scale. What is important is to allow a keen esthetic appreciation of the qualities of the English Roses to determine the form of the arrangement. These few suggestions are intended only as a general guide to arrangements with English Roses: I am confident that no lover of flowers walking round a garden will find any lack of inspiration.

Left, a blue-and-white porcelain container holds a marvelous profusion of delphiniums, lilies and roses – among them 'The Alexandra Rose' and 'Sharifa Asma' – with sprays of a Rambler Rose to give the arrangement width. Above, a scheme of yellows and greens includes Achillea, *with its fern-like foliage.*

Varieties of the English Rose

There are now over eighty different varieties of English Roses. Together they represent the best from nearly thirty years of selective breeding. The following detailed portraits indicate not just the color, but also the size, shape and fragrance of each of these shrub roses, making it simple to choose a rose that would enhance any garden, whether large or small.

In my descriptions in this chapter, I have taken pains to provide a fair assessment of each rose. It is important to remember that the photographs only illustrate the rose at the moment the picture was taken. As the flower unfolds, it is continually changing its shape and color. If there appears to be some discrepancy between the photograph and the rose you see in the garden, I hope that my notes will clarify this.

As well as providing guidance on the esthetic qualities of the English Roses, I have included notes on such practical matters as health, vigor, habit of growth and foliage. I have endeavoured to be as frank as possible in relation to the virtues and defects of my roses. Over the years much progress has been made and it is inevitable that some varieties will score higher points than others in certain respects. A few earlier varieties have been dropped from our lists because they have been superseded by newer and better varieties. If a rose is noted here as having a weakness – for example, "a slight susceptibility to mildew" – that is not necessarily a reason for it to be disregarded. If that were so, we should not grow any roses at all. Instead, it should be taken as a warning against growing this rose in a garden that is particularly subject to mildew. In every other way, it may be an excellent plant. Similarly, some roses may have magnificent flowers but less satisfactory growth. 'The Squire,' for example, bears

Two English Roses with very different characters: 'L.D. Braithwaite' (opposite) in a late-summer arrangement, and 'Cymbeline' (above), with flowers of greyish-pink.

some of the most superb blooms of any rose I know; in contrast its growth is poor. Many rose growers would be happy to put up with this in order to enjoy flowers of such beauty and perfection.

Whatever their individual characteristics, all the English Roses are beautiful and many of them make graceful shrubs which flower longer than other garden plants. When making a choice for your garden, try to have a clear idea as to where the rose is to be placed. Consider not only its flowers and their color, but also its habit of growth, foliage and particular requirements. To simplify selection and for extra clarity, I have provided notes on such key features.

OVERALL ASSESSMENT

Each variety has been graded, according to my view of its overall virtue, thus:

*** VERY GOOD
** GOOD
* BELOW AVERAGE

This should in no way be taken as the last word on the subject – it is only intended as a very general assessment. Sometimes I give a rose only one or two stars simply because it does not, to me, wholly fulfil the requirements for an English Rose; although it may still be a very good plant. Lower-graded varieties may have virtues which are suitable for certain purposes, or which satisfy certain special needs or tastes.

FRAGRANCE

Some sort of guidance on fragrance can also be very useful. For this I have used a similar grading:

*** VERY GOOD
** GOOD
* BELOW AVERAGE

As I have said before (page 44), scent is elusive in roses, and can vary greatly according to temperature, time of day and other circumstances. My scale should be accurate under favorable conditions.

SHAPE AND DIMENSIONS

When planting, it is important to have some idea as to the ultimate dimensions we can expect a variety to achieve. Under each rose, a simple schematic diagram indicates the overall shape and habit of the rose. The roses are divided into four categories: bushy, spreading, arching or upright, with a diagram for each; the diagrams do not reflect the exact proportions of the plant. Dimensions are given alongside, but will not always be exact, for the ultimate size of a rose will vary according to the soil and climate in which the plant is growing. I have found that in southern Europe, the southern United States, California, Pacific Northwest and countries of the southern hemisphere, the English Roses tend to grow much larger.

RECOMMENDED GROUPING

I regard the planting of English Roses in groups, rather than singly, wherever space allows, as being of prime importance (see pages 50–1 and 146–7). This creates a much better effect and is well worth the extra investment. The numbers quoted are only suggestions – there is in fact no limit to the number of roses that can be planted together in a group.

My recommended figures may be taken as the minimum where space allows. However, where cost is a consideration or space is limited, single bushes are quite satisfactory.

STRAIN

"Strain" refers to the group within the English Roses to which the rose belongs (see pages 30–1).

BREEDING

In the notes on parentage, the mother parent comes first, the pollen parent second. In the case of 'Cottage Rose,' for example, we have 'Wife of Bath' (mother parent) × 'Mary Rose' (pollen parent). Occasionally the word "seedling" occurs – this simply means that we have taken an unnamed seedling from our breeding program and used it as a parent. A "sport" refers to a mutation in the genetic make-up of the plant, which produces a variation; an example is the white 'Winchester Cathedral,' which is a sport of the pink 'Mary Rose.' In every way except color, it is identical.

In the rose entries a classification is given for all varieties that are not English Roses; HT (Hybrid Tea) 'Monique,' for example. Throughout, I have used the term "variety" rather than the term "cultivar."

APPELLATION

The appellation is an international code name, as for example: 'Abraham Darby' (Auscot). The appellation is never actually used either in commerce or in the garden, but it is required by law to be placed alongside the proper names of all patented roses. The idea is that should the rose be given a different name in another country, it will always be recognizable. Roses, however, do not need to be patented, so it is often the case that no appellation is listed.

'Gertrude Jekyll' is an excellent English Rose, closely related to the Portland Roses. Its sumptuous, clear pink flowers have a particularly strong "Old Rose" fragrance.

Abraham Darby (LEFT)

This variety is unique among the English Roses in having Modern Rose parentage. It is a cross between the Modern Climber 'Aloha' and a yellow Floribunda, both of which parents bear flowers characteristic of an Old Rose. The flowers of ABRAHAM DARBY are of classic Old Rose shape, while still displaying something of the stamp of a Modern Rose. The beautiful cupped blooms are coppery apricot in color, with the outer petals turning more towards pink. The fragrance is very strong.

ABRAHAM DARBY forms a well-rounded shrub of dense growth, which is studded all over with bloom when in full flower; the foliage is plentiful and shiny. It repeats with remarkable regularity and is very vigorous and healthy (rugged enough to be trained as a climber), although susceptible to a touch of rust in some gardens. Because of its size and color, it is an ideal rose for the center of a flower arrangement. It was named after a founder of the Industrial Revolution for the Ironbridge Gorge Museum Trust.

OVERALL ASSESSMENT ***	FRAGRANCE ***
STRAIN 'ALOHA'	BREEDING FLORIBUNDA 'YELLOW CUSHION' × MODERN CLIMBER 'ALOHA'
APPELLATION AUSCOT	DATE OF INTRODUCTION 1985

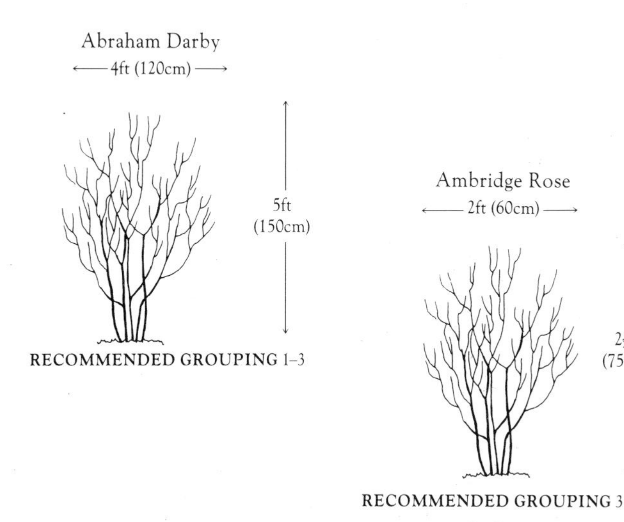

AMBRIDGE ROSE

Ambridge Rose (ABOVE)

This is a short, bushy little rose of comparatively low growth. It is particularly useful for smaller gardens and when placed towards the front of larger borders, or for growing as a bedding rose. The flowers are medium-sized and apricot-pink in color, becoming a very soft pale pink towards the edges; at first they are of neat, cupped formation, later opening out into a very attractive rosette. AMBRIDGE ROSE, which was named at the request of the BBC for their ever-popular radio serial "The Archers," is a tough, free-flowering and altogether trouble-free rose.

OVERALL ASSESSMENT **	FRAGRANCE ***
STRAIN 'WIFE OF BATH'	BREEDING 'CHARLES AUSTIN' × SEEDLING (PROBABLY 'WIFE OF BATH')
APPELLATION AUSWONDER	DATE OF INTRODUCTION 1990

Belle Story

This interesting rose brings a rather different form of flower to the English Roses. The petals are held slightly apart from each other and incurve towards their edges. The flower is neatly rounded and the yellow stamens at the center are clearly visible. The color is a delicate pink, fading slightly towards the edge of the petals. BELLE STORY, named after one of the first nursing sisters to serve as a British Royal Navy officer, forms a strong and reliable shrub and was rated "excellent" by the American Rose Society.

OVERALL ASSESSMENT **	FRAGRANCE **
STRAIN —	BREEDING ('CHAUCER' × MODERN CLIMBER 'PARADE') × ('THE PRIORESS' × FLORIBUNDA 'ICEBERG')
APPELLATION AUSELLE	DATE OF INTRODUCTION 1984

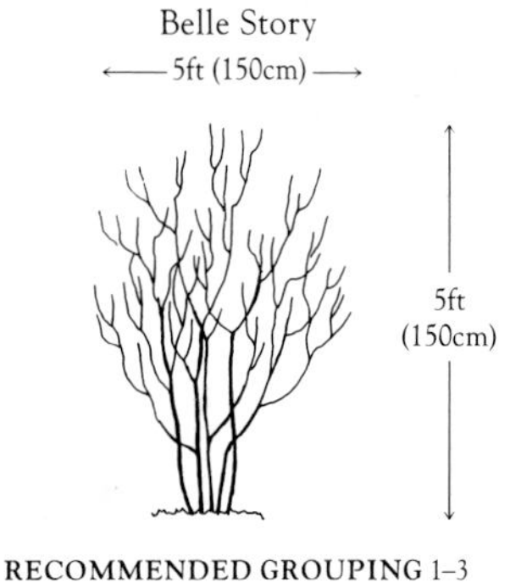

RECOMMENDED GROUPING 1–3

Bibi Maizoon (BELOW)

At its best, BIBI MAIZOON has a bloom which is hard to equal among English or Old Roses. The flowers are superb: large, globe-shaped and a clear, warm pink in color, rather like an improved Centifolia; they have a wonderful fragrance. Since its introduction in 1989 this variety has proved a little variable in its performance, and occasionally its flowers, though still beautiful, may be no more than shallowly cupped. This rose may also be a little slow to bloom: do not expect too many flowers in the first year, for it may need a full season's growth to show its true merit. Once it has built up a framework of seasoned growth, it forms an elegant, spreading, arching little shrub, with flowers hanging slightly on the branch.

BIBI MAIZOON

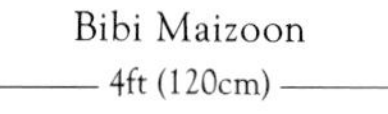

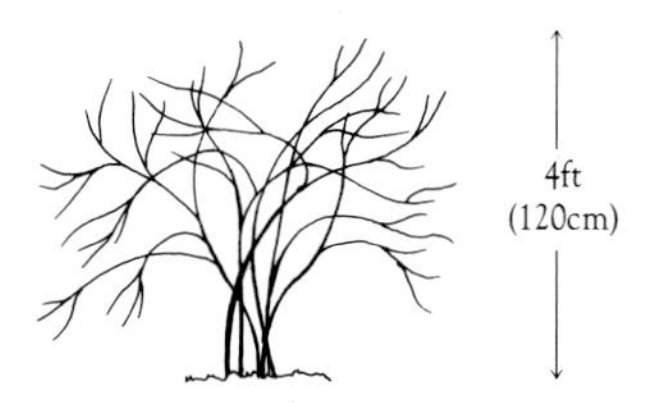

RECOMMENDED GROUPING 3

OVERALL ASSESSMENT **	FRAGRANCE ***
STRAIN 'OLD ROSE'	BREEDING 'THE REEVE' × 'CHAUCER'
APPELLATION AUSDIMINDO	DATE OF INTRODUCTION 1989

RECOMMENDED GROUPING 1–3

Bow Bells (ABOVE)

This excellent variety has much in common with Modern Shrub Roses. The small- to medium-sized cupped flowers are carried in Floribunda-like sprays throughout the summer. The flowers themselves show true English Rose character, their round bell-shaped petals producing a charming effect. The growth is vigorous and healthy, forming a broad, bushy plant which has good "modern" foliage.

OVERALL ASSESSMENT **	FRAGRANCE *
STRAIN —	BREEDING ('CHAUCER' × RUGOSA 'CONRAD FERDINAND MEYER') × 'GRAHAM THOMAS'
APPELLATION AUSBELLS	DATE OF INTRODUCTION 1991

BROTHER CADFAEL

Bredon

BREDON is a short, bushy shrub that is both free-flowering and reliable. The flowers are of medium size, rosette shape and buff-yellow coloring, becoming paler towards the edge of the flower. They have a pronounced fresh fruit fragrance. This variety leans towards the Modern Rose in its foliage and overall character, but its size, reliability and excellent habit of growth make it a useful little rose for the small garden, for bedding or even perhaps as a low hedge.

OVERALL ASSESSMENT *	FRAGRANCE ***
STRAIN 'ALOHA'	BREEDING 'WIFE OF BATH' × 'LILIAN AUSTIN'
APPELLATION —	DATE OF INTRODUCTION 1984

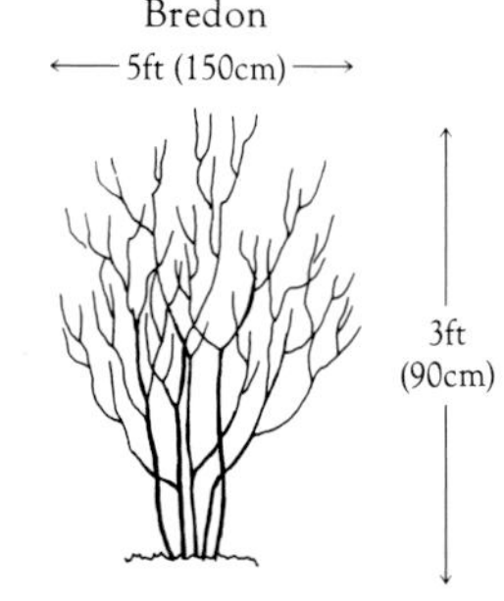
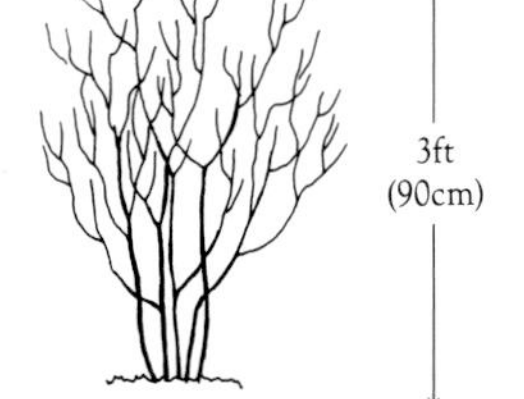

RECOMMENDED GROUPING 3

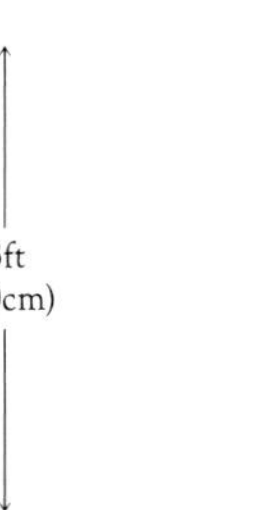

RECOMMENDED GROUPING 1–3

Brother Cadfael (OPPOSITE)

BROTHER CADFAEL has some of the largest and most sumptuous blooms of all the English Roses. The flowers are deeply cupped, with incurving petals giving a slightly enclosed effect; their color is a good medium pink. Despite their huge size, the blooms are never clumsy and remain crisp and fresh over a long period. They have an unusually strong fragrance. The flowers hang gracefully on the branch and are perfectly in proportion to the growth and foliage. Like ABRAHAM DARBY, BROTHER CADFAEL'S large bloom makes it an excellent candidate in the house for the center of a bowl of smaller flowers. The rose derives its name from a fictional character in the medieval novels of a Shropshire author.

OVERALL ASSESSMENT ***	FRAGRANCE ***
STRAIN 'GLOIRE DE DIJON'	BREEDING 'CHARLES AUSTIN' × SEEDLING
APPELLATION AUSGLOBE	DATE OF INTRODUCTION 1990

CANTERBURY

RECOMMENDED GROUPING 3–5

Canterbury (ABOVE RIGHT)

CANTERBURY is, in my opinion, one of the most beautiful of the single, or near single, roses, other than the Species Roses. (It is in fact a semi-double variety, though the impression is one of a single rose.) The flowers are large and open wide, with petals of a pure, translucent pink and a lovely, sheeny texture. Its growth is low and spreading, with not very plentiful foliage. As a shrub, it does not have great strength and for this reason is not widely grown, but it received a "good" rating from the American Rose Society.

OVERALL ASSESSMENT *	FRAGRANCE **
STRAIN —	BREEDING (HT 'MONIQUE' × 'CONSTANCE SPRY') × SEEDLING
APPELLATION —	DATE OF INTRODUCTION 1969

Cardinal Hume

Although this rose was originally bred by Harkness and Co. of Hitchin, I have, at their suggestion, included it among the English Roses as it has so many of the characteristics of an English Rose. It is a shrub of almost ideal habit of growth, the branches arching out to perfection and forming a lovely, low mound. The flowers, which are a rich, dark purple in color and a little smaller than medium size, are held in sprays; they have a fruit-like fragrance. Whereas they do not have typical Old Rose shape, they are produced with great freedom – few roses repeat-flower so regularly. The one weakness of this variety is a tendency to blackspot, which means that in areas subject to this disease spraying is essential.

OVERALL ASSESSMENT **	FRAGRANCE **
STRAIN —	BREEDING ((SEEDLING × (FLORIBUNDA 'ORANGE SENSATION' × FLORIBUNDA 'ALLGOLD') × *R. CALIFORNICA*)) × MODERN SHRUB 'FRANK NAYLOR'
APPELLATION HARREGALE	DATE OF INTRODUCTION 1984

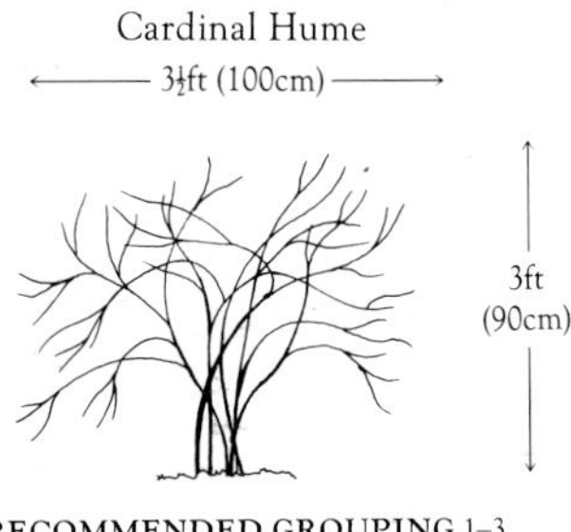

RECOMMENDED GROUPING 1–3

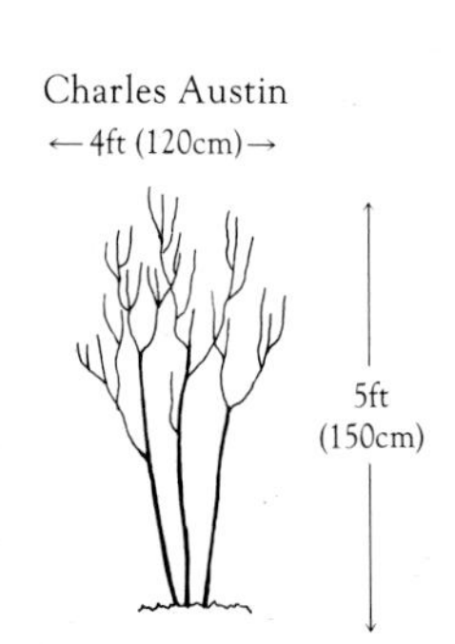

RECOMMENDED GROUPING 3

OVERALL ASSESSMENT *	FRAGRANCE **
STRAIN 'ALOHA'	BREEDING 'CHAUCER' × MODERN CLIMBER 'ALOHA'
APPELLATION —	DATE OF INTRODUCTION 1973

CHARLES AUSTIN

Charles Austin (ABOVE)

A popular rose when it was introduced in the early years of the English Roses, CHARLES AUSTIN produces some fine, very large blooms which are often much appreciated by flower arrangers. The blooms are cup-shaped and of varying shades of apricot, later fading. They have a strong fresh-fruit fragrance. CHARLES AUSTIN requires pruning to at least half its height if it is not to become too tall and ungainly. Its foliage is very large and "modern" in appearance. It does not always repeat-flower well. Named after my father, this rose has one yellow sport, YELLOW CHARLES AUSTIN, introduced in 1981.

Charles Rennie Mackintosh (BELOW)

The distinctive feature of this rose is its color, which may vary, according to the weather and other conditions, from a dusky lilac-pink to a very definite lilac. It is an ideal shade for juxtaposing between plants, and particularly English Roses, of other colors, either in the border or a flower arrangement. The rose's cupped flowers have a strong fragrance, and feature smaller, inner petals that twist to give most attractive effects; flowering continues with great freedom up to late summer. The growth is vigorous and bushy with plentiful, thin, wiry stems and numerous, spiky thorns; the dark green leaves are quite small for an English Rose. Named after the famous Art Nouveau designer and architect, CHARLES RENNIE MACKINTOSH is a popular rose that has proved to be both tough and reliable.

OVERALL ASSESSMENT ***	FRAGRANCE **
STRAIN 'MARY ROSE'	BREEDING ('CHAUCER' × RUGOSA 'CONRAD FERDINAND MEYER') × 'MARY ROSE'
APPELLATION AUSREN	DATE OF INTRODUCTION 1988

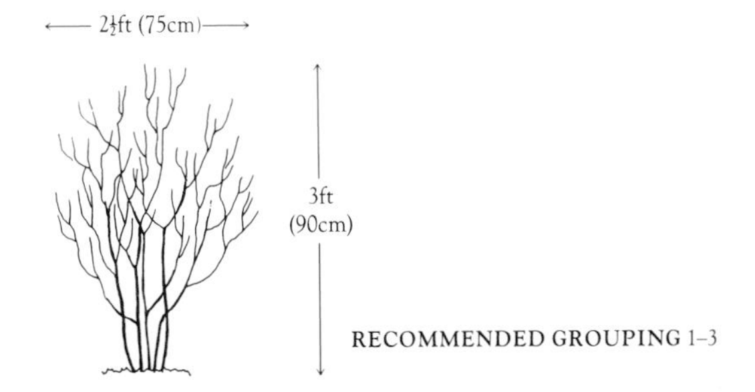

Charmian (ABOVE)

CHARMIAN carries large, heavy flowers, of a deep pink color, which weigh down its broad, arching growth. The rosette-shaped flowers open flat at first, the petals eventually recurving at the edges. There is a very powerful "Old Rose" fragrance. This rose has a rather floppy habit of growth, so when grown as a border or free-standing shrub needs to be planted in a group of two or more. If trained on a wall or up a free-standing support, it will make a useful short climber of perhaps 6 feet (2 meters). Alternatively, it will, if allowed, sprawl in a pleasing way over a low retaining wall.

OVERALL ASSESSMENT **	FRAGRANCE ***
STRAIN 'ALOHA'	BREEDING SEEDLING × 'LILIAN AUSTIN'
APPELLATION —	DATE OF INTRODUCTION 1982

Chaucer (BELOW)

CHAUCER has fine, deeply cupped, rose-pink flowers of classic Old Rose character. They have a strong fragrance of myrrh. The growth is upright and bushy, with matt-textured leaves of a light to medium green. It sometimes suffers from mildew. CHAUCER was one of our earliest introductions and is a parent of many of our better varieties.

OVERALL ASSESSMENT *	FRAGRANCE ***
STRAIN 'OLD ROSE'	BREEDING GALLICA 'DUCHESSE DE MONTEBELLO' × 'CONSTANCE SPRY'
APPELLATION —	DATE OF INTRODUCTION 1970

Chianti (BELOW)

OVERALL ASSESSMENT ***	FRAGRANCE ***
STRAIN 'OLD ROSE'	BREEDING FLORIBUNDA 'DUSKY MAIDEN' × GALLICA 'TUSCANY'
APPELLATION —	DATE OF INTRODUCTION 1967

One of the main foundation parents of the red varieties of English Roses, CHIANTI forms a fine, broad and vigorous shrub, bearing large Gallica-like flowers of a rich crimson that soon turns to a purplish-maroon. A cross between repeat- and summer-flowering parents, it is itself only summer-flowering, but then produces a massive display of fine blooms worthy of comparison with the very best of the Old Roses. It has a powerful 'Old Rose' fragrance. (For details of its breeding, see page 25.)

RECOMMENDED GROUPING 1

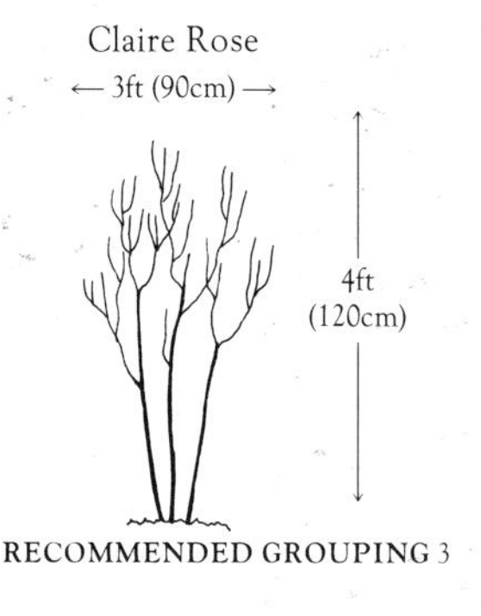

RECOMMENDED GROUPING 3

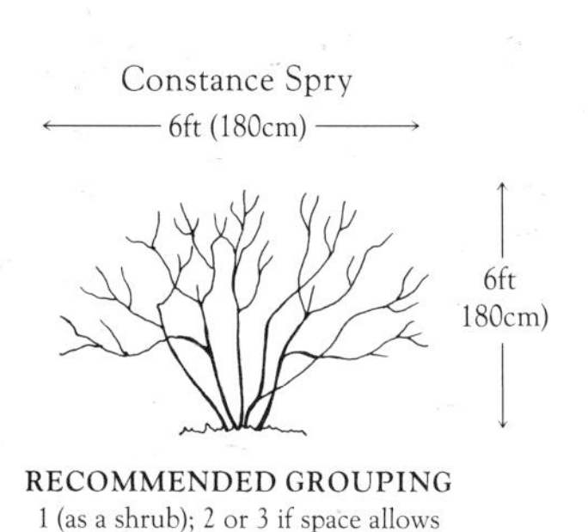

RECOMMENDED GROUPING
1 (as a shrub); 2 or 3 if space allows

Claire Rose (ABOVE)

At their best, the blooms of CLAIRE ROSE are large, magnificent and often of superb quality. A delicate blush-pink at first, fading with age, they open by stages to a flat rosette which eventually recurves slightly. There is a strong fragrance. The growth is unusually vigorous and upright, making it a good shrub for the back of the border behind other plants and roses; but it can look a little ungainly when on its own. It has close similarities to CHARLES AUSTIN. This variety has proved a little disappointing in Britain because its flowers spot in rain. In warmer, drier climates, I would expect no such problem.

OVERALL ASSESSMENT *	FRAGRANCE **
STRAIN 'ALOHA'	**BREEDING** 'CHARLES AUSTIN' × (SEEDLING × 'ICEBERG')
APPELLATION AUSLIGHT	**DATE OF INTRODUCTION** 1986

Constance Spry (RIGHT)

CONSTANCE SPRY is the original English Rose that caused such great interest when it was introduced by Graham Thomas in 1961 (through Sunningdale Nurseries). Being a cross between a repeat-flowering and a non-repeat-flowering rose, it flowers once only in early summer, with no later blooms. Its extremely large, cupped flowers, of a lovely soft pink, are some of the finest and largest "Old Rose" blooms of any variety. They have a strong myrrh fragrance – when first introduced there had been no other rose with this fragrance since the days of the old Ayrshire Roses.

A rose of large, unruly growth, CONSTANCE SPRY can be difficult to control in a small space. It is a good idea to train it on an encircling support or a low garden fence; alternatively, it can be grown as a climber, when it will reach a height of at least 12 feet (4 meters) and be covered in giant blooms in season (see also page 24). However it is grown, it will provide a magnificent display. It was named after Constance Spry (1886–1960), a pioneer in flower arrangement and one of the first collectors of Old Roses in the early part of the twentieth century.

OVERALL ASSESSMENT ***	FRAGRANCE ***
STRAIN 'OLD ROSE'	**BREEDING** GALLICA 'BELLE ISIS' × FLORIBUNDA 'DAINTY MAID'
APPELLATION —	**DATE OF INTRODUCTION** 1961

Cottage Rose

A charming and unassuming little rose of excellent garden habit, COTTAGE ROSE has a quite remarkable capacity to repeat-flower throughout the summer. The flowers are medium-sized, shallowly cupped rosettes of a pure, glowing pink. They have great charm, but only a light "Old Rose" fragrance. The growth is rather upright, sending out numerous small flowering branches, making it an ideal rose for a very small garden.

OVERALL ASSESSMENT ***	FRAGRANCE *
STRAIN 'WIFE OF BATH'	**BREEDING** 'WIFE OF BATH' × 'MARY ROSE'
APPELLATION AUSGLISTEN	**DATE OF INTRODUCTION** 1991

Cottage Rose

← 2½ft (75cm) →

3ft (90cm)

RECOMMENDED GROUPING 1–3

Country Living

COUNTRY LIVING is in many ways the epitome of an English Rose. It may not stand out as a particularly striking plant in the garden, being a rather modest rose, but it has many of the characteristics that I look for in our roses. The flower is very close to the ideal of an Old Rose. The petals are numerous, small and closely packed, forming a perfect rosette in shape. They are soft blush-pink in color, fading to palest pink. At the center there is often an attractive green eye, no more than a speck but rounding off the picture to perfection. Its growth is short, bushy and twiggy with small leaves. The whole effect is of a good, compact shrub, which is ideally suited to small gardens or to more intimate positions in larger gardens. A slight tendency to die-back in winter, inherited from its parent WIFE OF BATH, can be largely ignored, as the rose can nearly always be relied upon to shoot up again without ill effects. It was named for the magazine *Country Living*, which has long been an enthusiastic supporter of English Roses.

OVERALL ASSESSMENT ***	FRAGRANCE *
STRAIN 'WIFE OF BATH'	BREEDING 'WIFE OF BATH' × 'GRAHAM THOMAS'
APPELLATION AUSCOUNTRY	DATE OF INTRODUCTION 1991

Cressida (RIGHT)

This is a very large rose, both in growth and flower. Its mother parent, the Rugosa Rose 'Conrad Ferdinand Meyer,' is itself extremely strong and tall, and much of the same growth has been passed on to CRESSIDA. As a consequence it sends up huge, thick, thorny stems from the base, to form a large Rugosa-like shrub with big, rough-textured leaves. The flowers, despite their size, have a delicate appearance, being loosely cupped and filled with crinkled petals. They are soft apricot-pink in the center, graduating to palest pink on the outer petals. It has an exceptionally strong myrrh fragrance.

This variety can be rather shy in its production of blooms, although at its best it will give two crops of the most beautiful flowers. It really needs to be given space to grow without too much pruning, and it is one of those roses that are just as satisfactory, or perhaps even better, when used as a climber.

OVERALL ASSESSMENT **	FRAGRANCE ***
STRAIN —	BREEDING RUGOSA 'CONRAD FERDINAND MEYER' × 'CHAUCER'
APPELLATION —	DATE OF INTRODUCTION 1983

CRESSIDA

RECOMMENDED GROUPING 1–3

Cymbeline (OPPOSITE)

CYMBELINE forms a large, graceful arching shrub that is very similar in growth and flower to LUCETTA. The main difference is its most unusual gray-pink color, which is quite unlike that of any other rose I know. Like the mauve and lilac varieties, this rose is excellent for combining in color schemes both in the border and as a cut flower. Its flowers are not of typical Old Rose shape; they open wide, flat and are loosely semi-double. They are large – often measuring 5in (12cm) across – and have a strong myrrh fragrance. The photograph here shows the bloom at the half-open stage.

OVERALL ASSESSMENT **	FRAGRANCE ***
STRAIN 'HERITAGE'	BREEDING SEEDLING × 'LILIAN AUSTIN'
APPELLATION —	DATE OF INTRODUCTION 1982

Dove

The most pleasing aspect of this rose is its elegant habit of growth, which is low and spreading, with its flowers presented on slightly drooping branches. It has dark, pointed leaves of typical HERITAGE character. There is some tendency to blackspot. The blooms are the nearest to those of a Hybrid Tea to be found among the English Roses, but they open to form a flower rather of the character of a camellia, providing beauty in both bud and open flower. Their color is very pale pink, turning almost to white – an almost washed-out shade. There is a fragrance of fresh apple.

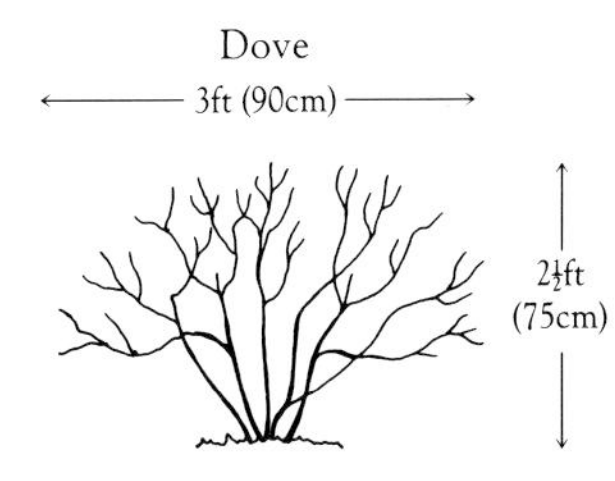

RECOMMENDED GROUPING 1–3

OVERALL ASSESSMENT *	FRAGRANCE **
STRAIN 'HERITAGE'	**BREEDING** 'WIFE OF BATH' × SEEDLING FROM FLORIBUNDA 'ICEBERG'
APPELLATION —	**DATE OF INTRODUCTION** 1984

CYMBELINE

Ellen

This rose has huge, rather loosely shaped cups of deep apricot coloring, with a very strong fragrance. Like CHARLES AUSTIN, the growth is upright, but broader and more bushy with large leaves. It is not a rose of great refinement, but it makes a good bold display in the border.

OVERALL ASSESSMENT *	FRAGRANCE ***
STRAIN 'ALOHA'	BREEDING 'CHARLES AUSTIN' × SEEDLING
APPELLATION —	DATE OF INTRODUCTION 1984

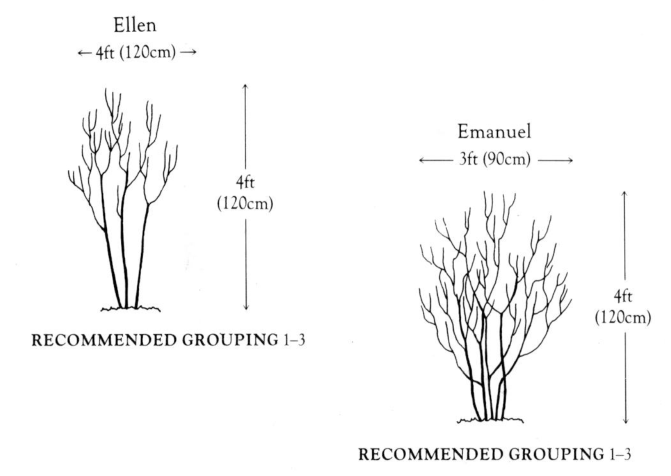

Emanuel (RIGHT)

This rose produces large, heavy, voluptuous flowers of soft blush-pink coloring, shaded with gold at the base of the petals. Opening wide, and bending back a little towards the end of their life, they can be as much

OVERALL ASSESSMENT *	FRAGRANCE ***
STRAIN 'HERITAGE'	BREEDING ('CHAUCER' × MODERN CLIMBER 'PARADE') × (SEEDLING × FLORIBUNDA 'ICEBERG')
APPELLATION —	DATE OF INTRODUCTION 1985

EMANUEL

as 12cm (5in) across. Despite their great size, they are produced with great freedom, and hang elegantly on their stems to face you; they are richly fragrant. The growth is vigorous and the leaves plentiful and dark. This would be one of our very best varieties were it not for its tendency to blackspot. Regular spraying can prevent the problem, but in areas subject to this disease, EMANUEL would perhaps be better avoided. This rose was named on behalf of David and Elizabeth Emanuel, the couturiers who designed the wedding dress for Lady Diana Spencer's marriage to the Prince of Wales in 1981.

EMILY

Emily (RIGHT)

This charming rose has flowers of unique formation. They start off as dainty little cups of soft pink buds; the outer petals then fall back flat, leaving the center of the flower cupped. Later the inner petals open to form a rosette and the outer petals fall back further, providing what is in effect a third formation. Eventually the whole flower becomes a rosette. Throughout this process the outer petals remain much paler in color, thereby emphasizing the changing forms. At all stages the flower is delightful, and has a strong fragrance. The bloom shown here is not quite typical: we would normally expect flat outer petals. The growth is short, upright and not very bushy. Although not all that it might be in terms of vigor, EMILY is so beautiful that I am loathe to exclude it from my list of English Roses. It needs rich soil and ample fertilizer and, if given the right treatment, will prove a useful rose for small gardens.

OVERALL ASSESSMENT **	FRAGRANCE ***
STRAIN 'WIFE OF BATH'	**BREEDING** 'THE PRIORESS' × 'MARY ROSE'
APPELLATION AUSBURTON	**DATE OF INTRODUCTION** 1992

English Elegance

This rose forms a large shrub of slightly arching growth which, as the name suggests, lends it a certain elegance. The flowers are large but not heavy, and nicely poised upon the branch. They open wide with loosely arranged inner petals enclosed within a ring of more formally arranged outer petals. The inner petals are in a great variety of tints, ranging from pink and salmon to copper, while the outer petals are of a softer pink. This mixture of colors provides a delightful, almost autumnal, effect. Although not a widely distributed shrub, and with really only two periods of bloom, it is good for borders, looking particularly well when arching over from the back of the border and mingling with other plants.

OVERALL ASSESSMENT **	FRAGRANCE *
STRAIN 'HERITAGE'	BREEDING NOT KNOWN
APPELLATION —	DATE OF INTRODUCTION 1986

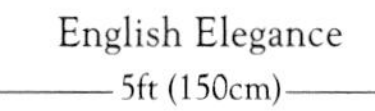

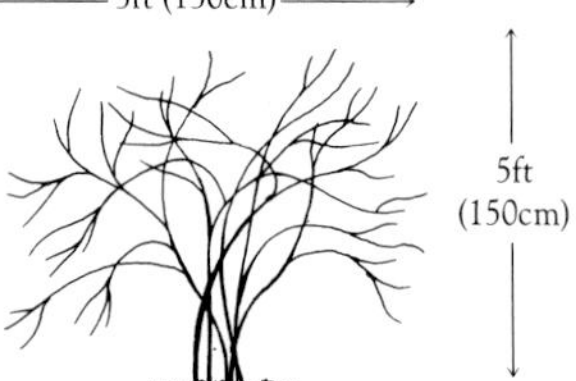

RECOMMENDED GROUPING 3

English Garden

OVERALL ASSESSMENT ***	FRAGRANCE *
STRAIN —	BREEDING ('LILIAN AUSTIN' × SEEDLING) × (FLORIBUNDA 'ICEBERG' × 'WIFE OF BATH')
APPELLATION AUSBUFF	DATE OF INTRODUCTION 1986

ENGLISH GARDEN bears flowers of perfect Old Rose formation. They open flat with numerous small petals, later becoming slightly domed; their color is yellow at the center, graduating almost to white on the outer petals. They have a light "Tea Rose" fragrance. This is quite a short plant with upright growth, not unlike a Hybrid Tea. This habit, if not ideal for the border, makes it suitable for a rose bed. Its leaves, as in many yellow roses, are pale green.

Evelyn (ABOVE)

EVELYN is a large and glorious rose. It is not an easy variety to describe, as its flowers vary so much both in shape and color. Their color is usually a glowing mixture of apricot and yellow with just a hint of pink, but at other times, particularly late in the season, it will be nearer to pure pink. Similarly, the shape is sometimes a broad, very shallow cup, with the petals turning up towards the edges; but otherwise forms more of a pure rosette. Whatever color or shape, the flowers are always pleasing, and their variations add greatly to the interest of the rose. EVELYN is a "sister" rose to JAYNE AUSTIN and SWEET JULIET, sharing some of the characteristics of both. However, it is shorter, producing more flowers and less growth. It makes a strong, upright, bushy shrub of medium height.

This variety has perhaps the strongest and most delicious fragrance of all the English Roses. The perfumers Crabtree & Evelyn chose this rose to represent their company.

OVERALL ASSESSMENT ***	FRAGRANCE ***
STRAIN 'GLOIRE DE DIJON'	BREEDING 'GRAHAM THOMAS' × 'TAMORA'
APPELLATION AUSSAUCER	DATE OF INTRODUCTION 1991

Fair Bianca (BELOW)

FAIR BIANCA has flowers of exquisite perfection – some of the most perfect of all the English Roses. Though not particularly large, they are of fully double rosette formation, with sometimes just a tinge of cream at the base of the petals. There is a strong myrrh fragrance. FAIR BIANCA will form a small shrub of upright, bushy growth, with rather sparse, light green foliage and numerous small thorns. It is close to an Old Rose both in flower and growth.

OVERALL ASSESSMENT **	FRAGRANCE ***
STRAIN 'OLD ROSE'	BREEDING NOT KNOWN
APPELLATION —	DATE OF INTRODUCTION 1982

Financial Times Centenary (ABOVE)

Perhaps the most notable feature of this rose is the wonderful clarity of its coloring – a pure, rich pink. (The half-open flower shown here does not have the purity of pink that would be more apparent at a later stage.) The flowers are quite deep and globular in shape; the petals incurve, partially enclosing their center. The growth of the plant may be said to be too upright to be ideal, but this is in fact an excellent rose for the back of the border. The shrub has large, dark green foliage and there is a rich "Old Rose" fragrance. Its name commemorates the 100th anniversary in 1988 of the *Financial Times*.

OVERALL ASSESSMENT *	FRAGRANCE ***
STRAIN —	BREEDING TWO UNNAMED SEEDLINGS
APPELLATION AUSFIN	DATE OF INTRODUCTION 1988

FISHERMAN'S FRIEND

RECOMMENDED GROUPING 3

Fisherman's Friend (ABOVE)

This rose is a deep garnet-crimson. Its fine, full-petalled flowers are cupped at first, later forming an attractive rosette; they have a powerful "Old Rose" fragrance. Its growth is strong. It may suffer from blackspot in Britain, but will withstand winters in Zone 5 and above better than most roses. The company Fisherman's Friend bought its name in an auction for the charity "Children in Need."

OVERALL ASSESSMENT *	FRAGRANCE ***
STRAIN 'THE SQUIRE'	BREEDING 'LILIAN AUSTIN' × 'THE SQUIRE'
APPELLATION AUSCHILD	DATE OF INTRODUCTION 1987

Francine Austin (RIGHT)

FRANCINE AUSTIN, like THE ALEXANDRA ROSE, is not usually classified as an English Rose. However, it is a descendant of an old variety – the excellent Noisette 'Alister Stella Gray' – and as it is sufficiently close to an English Rose in character, it is worth including here. In many respects it resembles a Ground-cover Rose, bearing small, white, pompon flowers in large, open sprays. The blooms themselves are very pretty

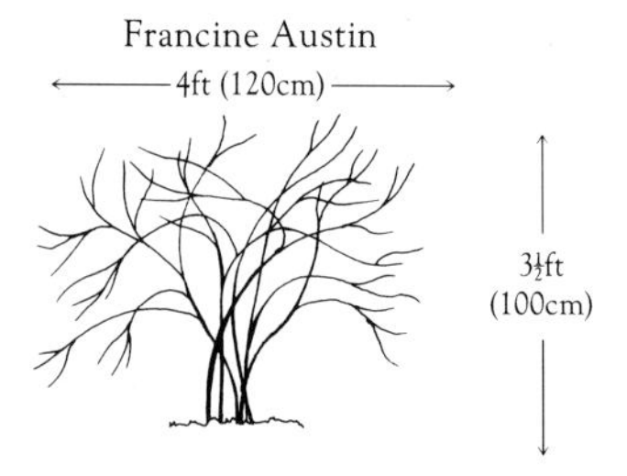

RECOMMENDED GROUPING 1, 3 or more

and are held on thin, wire-like stems, producing a dainty effect that makes them particularly useful for mixing with the larger and heavier English Roses, both in the border and in flower arrangements. The growth is excellent, forming an elegant, arching shrub. This variety has pale green leaves with long, narrow, widely spaced leaflets.

If allowed to grow unchecked, individual plants of FRANCINE AUSTIN can become large and open in habit; so where space allows it is probably better to grow the variety in a group to achieve a denser, bushier shrub. On the other hand, it can be pruned quite severely, encouraging new growth to appear annually from the base, to provide a smaller bush. Alternatively, plant it near a wall, where it will grow into a fine repeat-flowering climber. FRANCINE AUSTIN is an excellent garden shrub, named after my daughter-in-law.

OVERALL ASSESSMENT ***	FRAGRANCE *
STRAIN —	BREEDING NOISETTE 'ALISTER STELLA GRAY' × MODERN SHRUB 'BALLERINA'
APPELLATION AUSRAM	DATE OF INTRODUCTION 1988

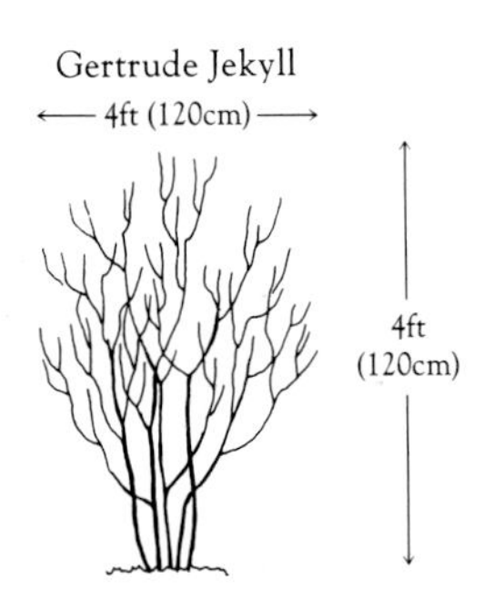

RECOMMENDED GROUPING 2 or 3

Gertrude Jekyll

GERTRUDE JEKYLL has magnificent, large, rich, warm pink flowers of true Old Rose shape. They begin as dainty, small buds, rather like those of the Alba Rose 'Celestial,' and then surprise us by opening out into rather heavy, rosette-shaped flowers with a strong affinity to the Portland Roses. GERTRUDE JEKYLL has an exceptionally powerful "Old Rose" fragrance; indeed, in recent experiments, carried out for the extraction of essential oil for perfume, this rose was found to be superior to any other. Since then it has been at least equalled in this respect by another English Rose, EVELYN. Its growth is exceptionally strong, perhaps at times even a little ungainly. The leaves are large with pointed leaflets, having something of the elegant character of a Damask Rose.

In the course of our search for good practical qualities in our English Roses – health, vigor, good repeat-flowering, etc. – we occasionally back-cross our existing varieties to Old Roses in order to recapture some small influence that we feel we may have lost. GERTRUDE JEKYLL is a cross between WIFE OF BATH and the beautiful old Portland Rose 'Comte de Chambord.' The latter shares, in many respects, the qualities of an English Rose, being of true Old Rose form and character, with a strong "Old Rose" fragrance and a capacity to repeat-flower.

This beautiful and very reliable rose was named after the gardener Gertrude Jekyll (1843–1932).

OVERALL ASSESSMENT ***	FRAGRANCE ***
STRAIN 'PORTLAND'	**BREEDING** 'WIFE OF BATH' × PORTLAND ROSE 'COMTE DE CHAMBORD'
APPELLATION AUSBORD	**DATE OF INTRODUCTION** 1986

Glamis Castle

2½ft (75cm)

3ft (90cm)

RECOMMENDED GROUPING 1–3

Glamis Castle

This outstanding rose has white flowers and dainty, bushy growth with light, twiggy branches. The flowers are deeply cupped with rather informally arranged petals; there is a strong myrrh fragrance. Being quite short, it is an ideal plant for small gardens, for the front of borders or for use as a bedding rose. It flowers with all the freedom and continuity of a Floribunda, while still retaining the true charm of an Old Rose, and its blooms produce a wonderful, airy effect in the mass. GLAMIS CASTLE takes its name from the Scottish seat of the Earls of Strathmore and Kinghorne – a royal residence since 1372, the childhood home of HM Queen Elizabeth The Queen Mother, the birthplace of HRH The Princess Margaret, and the setting for Shakespeare's *Macbeth*.

OVERALL ASSESSMENT ***	FRAGRANCE ***
STRAIN 'WIFE OF BATH'	**BREEDING** 'GRAHAM THOMAS' × 'MARY ROSE'
APPELLATION AUSLEVEL	**DATE OF INTRODUCTION** 1992

Golden Celebration

This variety shows every sign of being one of our finest and most popular roses to date. It has giant, incurved, cup-shaped blooms, held elegantly upon arching stems. The flowers are of a lovely coppery-yellow coloring, uncommon among roses and not hitherto found among the English Roses. If you look closely at the petals you will see that they achieve this color effect with minute dots of pink on a deep yellow background, though this would not usually be noticeable. The blooms have a powerful fragrance.

The growth and foliage is strong and remarkably resistant to disease. This is an excellent all-round rose, combining beauty, elegance and strength.

OVERALL ASSESSMENT ***	FRAGRANCE ***
STRAIN 'ALOHA'	BREEDING 'CHARLES AUSTIN' × 'ABRAHAM DARBY'
APPELLATION AUSGOLD	DATE OF INTRODUCTION 1992

Graham Thomas

Even after the introduction of many good, yellow roses – probably more than in any other color – this variety remains one of the most sought-after of all English Roses. There are good reasons for this: not only is it an excellent rose in every way, but also I can think of few roses, even among the Hybrid Teas, that have such pure, rich, yellow coloring. At their best, the flowers are of the most satisfactory cupped shape and have a delicious "Tea Rose" fragrance.

Graham Thomas
←4ft (120cm)→
5ft (150cm)

RECOMMENDED GROUPING 1–3

GRAHAM THOMAS has excellent growth, being very vigorous and freely branching, and producing its flowers with remarkable continuity throughout the summer. In the warmer climates of the world, it can even be a little too vigorous, sending up long climbing shoots that should be cut back if you wish to retain the rose's shrubby growth. One of the best of the English Roses, GRAHAM THOMAS has done much to enhance their popularity since it was introduced, together with MARY ROSE, at The Chelsea Flower Show in 1983. The American Rose Society has given GRAHAM THOMAS a "good" rating.

Graham Thomas, who chose this variety to bear his name, was the prime mover for the reintroduction of the Old Roses and may be said to have paved the way for the development of the English Roses.

OVERALL ASSESSMENT ***	FRAGRANCE ***
STRAIN 'HERITAGE'	BREEDING 'CHARLES AUSTIN' × (FLORIBUNDA 'ICEBERG' × SEEDLING)
APPELLATION AUSMAS	DATE OF INTRODUCTION 1983

Gruss an Aachen

Bred by F. Geduldig of Germany in 1909, this beautiful rose was the result of a cross between the famous old Hybrid Perpetual 'Frau Karl Druschki' and a Hybrid Tea. I have classified it here as an English Rose since it has so much in common with what I would regard as an ideal English Rose. The flowers are of perfect cupped Old Rose formation and they have a lovely, pearly pink color that fades with age to creamy white; they are strongly and deliciously fragrant. GRUSS AN AACHEN forms a hardy little bush with good disease-resistant foliage. There is also a climbing form.

OVERALL ASSESSMENT **	FRAGRANCE ***
STRAIN —	BREEDING HYBRID PERPETUAL 'FRAU KARL DRUSCHKI' × HT 'FRANZ DEEGEN'
APPELLATION —	DATE OF INTRODUCTION 1909

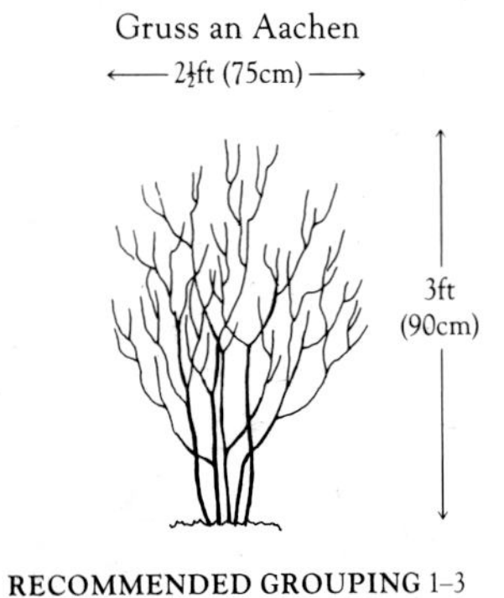

RECOMMENDED GROUPING 1–3

Heritage (RIGHT)

HERITAGE is one of the best and most popular of the English Roses. The blooms are of perfect cupped formation and of medium size; they are a very soft, clear pink at the center, while the outer petals are almost white. This is a flower of delicate shell-like beauty. Its fragrance is strong and pleasing, with a slight overtone of honey. The growth is equally satisfying, showing signs of its grandparent 'Iceberg,' with smooth rather "Musk Rose" foliage and clean stems with only a few thorns. It is strong and bushy, breaking freely from the stem and the base to produce further blooms. It has very good repeat-flowering properties and the American Rose Society has given it an "excellent" rating.

OVERALL ASSESSMENT ***	FRAGRANCE ***
STRAIN 'HERITAGE'	BREEDING SEEDLING × (FLORIBUNDA 'ICEBERG' × 'WIFE OF BATH')
APPELLATION AUSBLUSH	DATE OF INTRODUCTION 1984

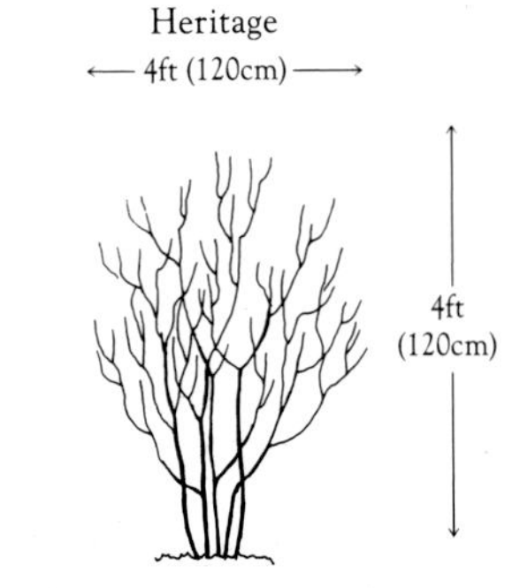

RECOMMENDED GROUPING 1–3

Hero (LEFT)

The exceptional feature of this rose is the pure, clear pink of its deep globe-shaped flowers. Later in the season the flowers, such as those illustrated here, are usually shallowly cupped. The blooms are widely spaced and held in sprays; they have a strong myrrh fragrance. The growth is tall and, by the standards of later varieties of English Roses, perhaps rather too open, with long, smooth stems, occasional thorns and sparse foliage. This is a rose that needs to be grown in a group of three or more, where it will combine to make one good shrub.

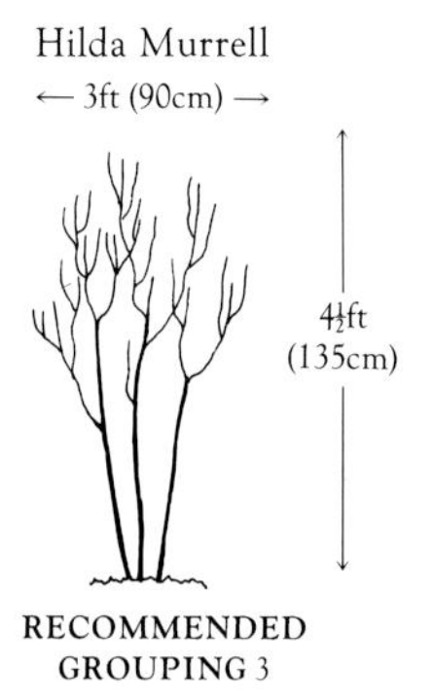

Hilda Murrell

We classify this rose as a "summer-flowering" variety. In warmer climates there may be a second crop of flowers, but this is unusual in Britain. Its beautiful flowers are an attractive rosette shape and have a wonderfully rich, glowing pink coloring. They open flat with numerous small petals and have a strong "Old Rose" fragrance. The foliage is ample and rough-textured, with very thorny stems, rather like a Rugosa Rose. The growth is robust and very upright. Hilda Murrell, after whom this rose was named just before her mysterious death in 1984, was an early pioneer for the reintroduction of Old Roses.

OVERALL ASSESSMENT **	FRAGRANCE ***
STRAIN 'HERITAGE'	BREEDING 'THE PRIORESS' × SEEDLING
APPELLATION —	DATE OF INTRODUCTION 1982

OVERALL ASSESSMENT *	FRAGRANCE ***
STRAIN 'THE SQUIRE'	BREEDING SEEDLING × (MODERN CLIMBER 'PARADE' × 'CHAUCER')
APPELLATION —	DATE OF INTRODUCTION 1984

Jayne Austin (BELOW)

Among the many excellent yellow and apricot varieties of English Rose – most of which relate back to the famous old Climbing Noisette 'Gloire de Dijon' – JAYNE AUSTIN, named after my daughter-in-law, is outstanding for its delicacy of flower and perfection of form. The petals have a silky, luminous texture which, together with their soft yellow coloring, gives the flower a charm that is hard to exaggerate. The flowers are of medium to large size, shallowly cupped at first, later becoming rosette shaped; they have a most delicious "Tea Rose" fragrance. The growth is rather upright and exceptionally robust, with plentiful shoots sprouting from the base of the plant. Like other yellow roses in this group, it has a tendency to send up long branches which, if left unpruned, may make the plant look a little ungainly. These growths should be cut back as they begin to mature to maintain a good, balanced overall shape. The foliage is plentiful and pale green, showing signs of its Noisette Rose ancestry.

OVERALL ASSESSMENT ***	FRAGRANCE ***
STRAIN 'GLOIRE DE DIJON'	BREEDING 'GRAHAM THOMAS' × 'TAMORA'
APPELLATION AUSBREAK	DATE OF INTRODUCTION 1990

Kathryn Morley

This beautiful rose is one of my favorites. The flowers are quite large and cupped in shape, though under less favorable conditions they may form a more shallow cup. They have a soft pink color. Although they do not display perfect symmetry, they have an informality that is particularly pleasing. I think it is the small intertwining petals at the center of the flower that gives them their appeal. The fragrance is strong under most conditions and hovers between myrrh and "Old Rose." The growth is vigorous and the blooms are held on long stems, which gives the plant an air of distinction. Mr and Mrs Eric Morley of the Variety Club of Great Britain bought the right to name this rose at a charity auction and named it after their daughter who died at the age of eighteen.

Kathryn Morley

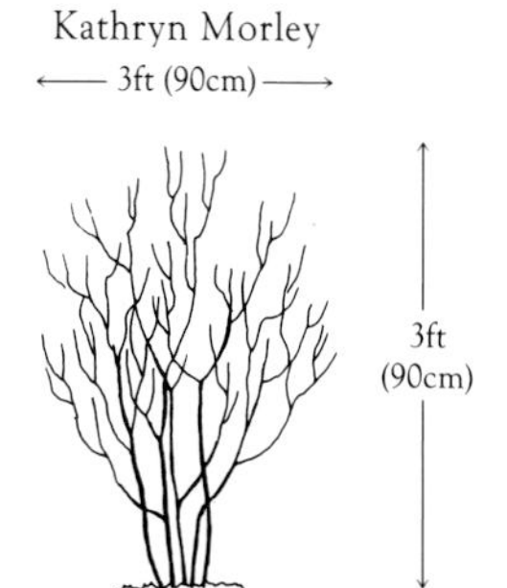

RECOMMENDED GROUPING 1–3

OVERALL ASSESSMENT ***	FRAGRANCE ***
STRAIN 'OLD ROSE'	BREEDING 'MARY ROSE' × 'CHAUCER'
APPELLATION AUSVARIETY	DATE OF INTRODUCTION 1990

L.D. Braithwaite

Good reds are notoriously hard to come by in any class of rose. This is a color that tends to fade easily in roses – and sometimes to a not altogether pleasing shade. L.D. BRAITHWAITE has the virtue of flowers of the brightest crimson among the English Roses, and a color that does not quickly fade. The flowers are attractive, if not of perfect Old Rose formation, opening wide to form a rather loose-petalled bloom. They are produced with remarkable continuity throughout the season – it is seldom that a group planting of this rose is without flowers. It has a fairly strong "Old Rose" fragrance. The growth is quite low, broad and open, making it a very satisfactory

RECOMMENDED GROUPING 3

rose for the garden. Resulting from a cross between MARY ROSE, which has excellent growth, and THE SQUIRE, which has poor growth but magnificent blooms, L.D. BRAITHWAITE has taken on the best characteristics of both parents. Though other English Roses may surpass it in quality of bloom, I regard this rose as the best garden variety of the red roses currently available. It was named after my father-in-law, Leonard Braithwaite.

OVERALL ASSESSMENT ***	FRAGRANCE **
STRAIN 'THE SQUIRE'	**BREEDING** 'MARY ROSE' × 'THE SQUIRE'
APPELLATION AUSCRIM	**DATE OF INTRODUCTION** 1988

Leander

A first class shrub of considerable proportions, LEANDER has deep apricot flowers, of less than medium size, borne in large, open sprays. The blooms are perfectly formed, the petals fanning out from the center in faultless symmetry. They are smaller and more exquisite than those of its parent CHARLES AUSTIN, but, like them, lack a true Old Rose softness. There is a strong, distinctly fruity fragrance. It is as a garden shrub that LEANDER comes into its own, forming an upright but by no means narrow shrub that is particularly useful in a border with other large plants. The growth is very vigorous; it has large, polished "modern" leaves and is almost entirely without disease. Although we usually classify LEANDER as an early summer-flowering rose, it is certainly capable of repeat-flowering, but this will be restricted to one or two long shoots from the base of the plant in autumn.

OVERALL ASSESSMENT ***	FRAGRANCE **
STRAIN 'ALOHA'	BREEDING 'CHARLES AUSTIN' × SEEDLING
APPELLATION —	DATE OF INTRODUCTION 1982

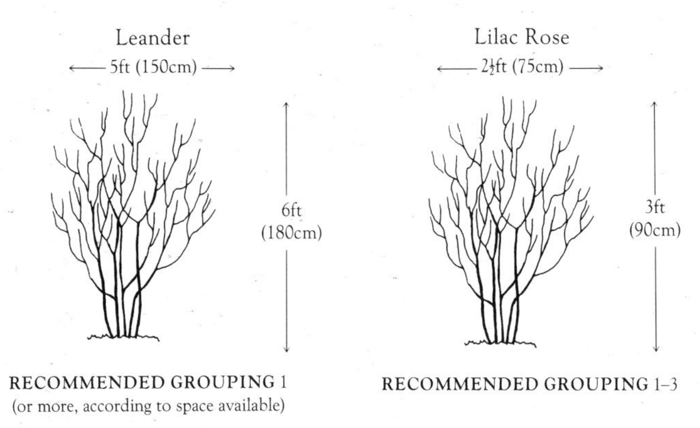

RECOMMENDED GROUPING 1
(or more, according to space available)

RECOMMENDED GROUPING 1–3

Lilac Rose

LILAC ROSE bears large, perfectly formed rosette-shaped flowers of a delicate lilac coloring. It has an exceptionally strong fragrance. This is a good rose to use in combination with varieties of other colors, especially towards the front of the border, where its color and rather flat-topped, short, bushy growth will fit in well with the plants around it.

OVERALL ASSESSMENT **	FRAGRANCE ***
STRAIN —	BREEDING SEEDLING × 'HERO'
APPELLATION AUSLILAC	DATE OF INTRODUCTION 1990

Lilian Austin (RIGHT)

LILIAN AUSTIN bears fragrant flowers of about 9cm (3½in) across, which open wide and rather informally. Salmon-pink in color with orange and apricot tints, the blooms are produced continually. A most useful and reliable variety, this rose has a "modern," but distinctly shrubby, appearance. It has strong, low, spreading growth, similar to that of a Ground-cover Rose. Though never unruly, its growth draws much from its parent 'Aloha.' It is an excellent rose to place along the front of a border where its spreading habit can be encouraged to make it flow over on to a path. Named after my mother who had a great love of flowers, LILIAN AUSTIN has proved to be an important "parent" and fully deserves the rating of "outstanding" given by the American Rose Society.

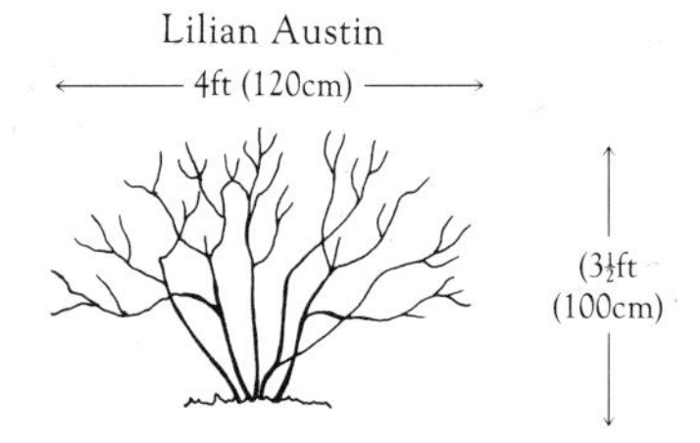

RECOMMENDED GROUPING 1, 3 or more

OVERALL ASSESSMENT ***	FRAGRANCE **
STRAIN 'ALOHA'	BREEDING MODERN CLIMBER 'ALOHA' × 'THE YEOMAN'
APPELLATION —	DATE OF INTRODUCTION 1973

Lucetta

LUCETTA is a rose of the HERITAGE strain, with long arching growth and large, polished leaves. The saucer-like flowers, 5in (12cm) across and a little more than semi-double, open flat and are of soft pink coloring, fading almost to white towards the end of their life. They have a nicely rounded, clean-cut appearance and a good fragrance. Planted in a group of three or more, this rose will form what is, in effect, one fine, elegant shrub. It is seldom without flowers and is in every way tough and reliable. The photograph shows the flower half open.

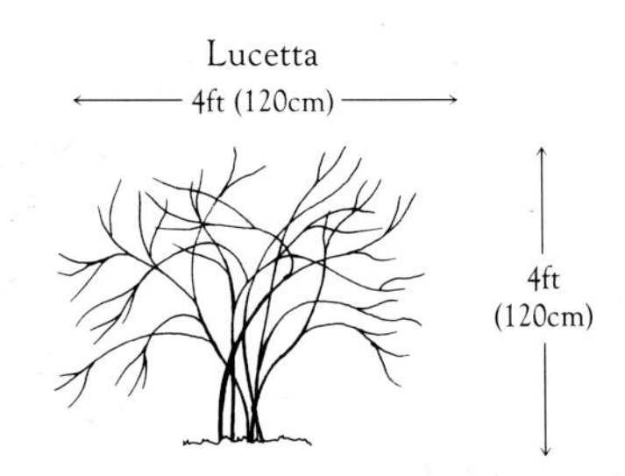

RECOMMENDED GROUPING 1, 3 or more

OVERALL ASSESSMENT **	FRAGRANCE ***
STRAIN 'HERITAGE'	**BREEDING** NOT KNOWN
APPELLATION —	**DATE OF INTRODUCTION** 1983

Mary Rose

MARY ROSE is a shrub with many remarkable qualities. Although not a particularly glamorous rose, it has virtues that make it a good all-round shrub. It is very continuous in bloom, starting early and finishing late, with little rest in between. Its growth is near to ideal – bushy, twiggy and vigorous without being unruly – and it has a remarkable resistance to disease. The blooms are a strong rose-pink in color and have a simple charm such as we associate with Old Roses. Though not especially shapely, being fairly loose-petalled in formation, they are nicely poised on the branch. The overall effect of the bush in the border is most attractive. The fragrance is only slight.

MARY ROSE has been widely used in our breeding program, bringing its many excellent qualities into our more recent introductions. It has also been a prolific producer of color sports, including the white WINCHESTER CATHEDRAL and the soft pink REDOUTÉ. Such color changes occur quite frequently among roses and when we happen to find a good example in our rose fields, it is immediately budded to provide a new variety. This rose was named on behalf of the Mary Rose Trust to mark the recovery of Henry VIII's famous flagship. The American Rose Society rated MARY ROSE as "excellent."

RECOMMENDED GROUPING 1–3

OVERALL ASSESSMENT ***	FRAGRANCE *
STRAIN 'MARY ROSE'	BREEDING 'WIFE OF BATH' × 'THE MILLER'
APPELLATION AUSMARY	DATE OF INTRODUCTION 1983

Mary Webb

MARY WEBB has very large, deeply cupped flowers with many petals. Of all shades of yellow to be found among roses, a soft lemon is perhaps the most pleasing and suitable. This rose has flowers of just such a color. They are borne on long stems and have a strong fragrance. The growth is vigorous, bushy and upright, with large, pale green leaves. Although not in the front rank of English Roses, this rose is superb under glass, as we discovered when forcing roses for The Chelsea Flower Show. This suggests to me that it might prove to be a good rose in warmer climates. It was named after the Shropshire novelist and poet, Mary Webb (1881–1927).

OVERALL ASSESSMENT *	FRAGRANCE ***
STRAIN 'ALOHA'	BREEDING SEEDLING × FLORIBUNDA 'CHINATOWN'
APPELLATION —	DATE OF INTRODUCTION 1984

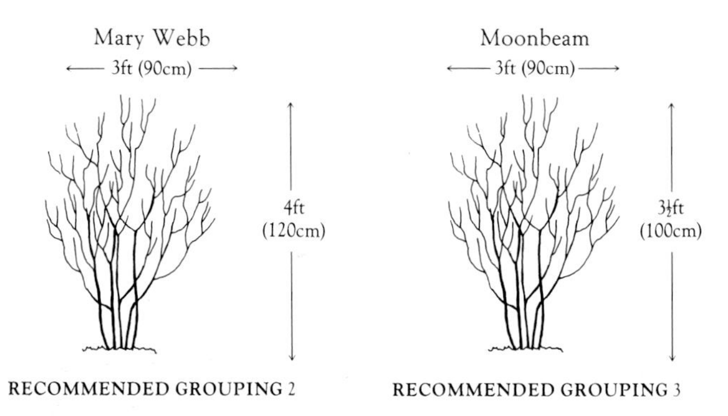

Moonbeam (BELOW)

MOONBEAM is more of a Modern Shrub Rose than a typical English Rose. It is, however, a reliable rose, bearing sprays of large semi-double flowers of pale apricot color. It is free-flowering and can be depended upon to make a fine display both early and late in the season.

OVERALL ASSESSMENT **	FRAGRANCE **
STRAIN —	BREEDING NOT KNOWN
APPELLATION —	DATE OF INTRODUCTION 1983

Othello (LEFT)

OTHELLO is a large, heavy rose of open cupped shape with numerous small petals in the hollow of the flower. The predominant color is a rather dusky crimson, but within its deep cups are all manner of tints ranging in tone from crimson to cerise and mauve. Pure crimson flowers, as illustrated here, frequently occur, but more often they are a mixture of hues. The flowers are held on stiff, upright stems and have a powerful "Old Rose" fragrance. The growth, though upright, is bushy with numerous thorns; the dark green leaves are thick and rough-textured. This is an unusual rose, which some might find a little coarse for their tastes, but it deserves to be appreciated for its unique character.

Othello
← 5ft (150cm) →
5ft (150cm)
RECOMMENDED GROUPING 3

OVERALL ASSESSMENT *	FRAGRANCE ***
STRAIN 'THE SQUIRE'	BREEDING 'LILIAN AUSTIN' × 'THE SQUIRE'
APPELLATION AUSLO	DATE OF INTRODUCTION 1986

Peach Blossom
← 3ft (90cm) →

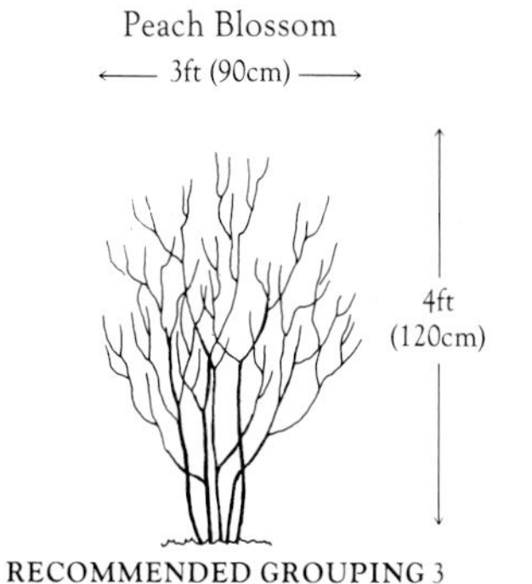

RECOMMENDED GROUPING 3

Peach Blossom

PEACH BLOSSOM produces a profusion of dainty, semi-double flowers of delicate blush coloring, on fairly upright, bushy growth. The individual flowers do not really resemble those of a peach as they are much larger, but there is certainly something blossom-like in the massed effect. Repeat-flowering is good, but you may choose to forego the later blooms in favor of the multitude of hips produced in autumn, if it is not dead-headed after its first flowering.

OVERALL ASSESSMENT **	FRAGRANCE **
STRAIN 'OLD ROSE'	BREEDING 'THE PRIORESS' × 'MARY ROSE'
APPELLATION AUSBLOSSOM	DATE OF INTRODUCTION 1990

Perdita (BELOW)

A member of the HERITAGE group, PERDITA is rather shorter than HERITAGE itself. It has darker foliage and forms a neat bush of medium size, but tends to be larger in mild US zones. The flowers begin as small, almost Hybrid Tea buds, opening at first cupped and later as a neat rosette. The bud is a soft pink at the center, with almost white outer petals. Later this turns blush-pink, flushed with yellow at the base of the petals. The fragrance is spicy: PERDITA was awarded a medal for fragrance by the British Royal National Rose Society in 1984.

OVERALL ASSESSMENT ***	FRAGRANCE ***
STRAIN 'HERITAGE'	BREEDING 'THE FRIAR' × (SEEDLING × FLORIBUNDA 'ICEBERG'
APPELLATION —	DATE OF INTRODUCTION 1983

PRETTY JESSICA

RECOMMENDED GROUPING 3–5

PERDITA

RECOMMENDED GROUPING 3 or more

Pretty Jessica (ABOVE)

This is a short, compact variety that bears true Old Rose flowers, opening from pretty little cups to form attractive rosettes. The color is a lovely rich, clear pink, and there is a strong "Old Rose" fragrance. This rose has enjoyed considerable popularity, partly for its classic Old Rose character and partly because its short, bushy growth makes it valuable for very small gardens. Unfortunately, it is not very resistant to disease and soon loses its foliage, but with adequate spraying it is a very worthwhile little rose.

OVERALL ASSESSMENT *	FRAGRANCE ***
STRAIN 'OLD ROSE'	BREEDING 'WIFE OF BATH' × SEEDLING
APPELLATION —	DATE OF INTRODUCTION 1983

Prospero (RIGHT)

PROSPERO bears flowers of the most perfect symmetry; seldom is there a petal out of place. They are of domed rosette shape with numerous small petals and deep crimson coloring, becoming a rich shade of purple with age. The growth is on the short side, not very robust, but with suitable feeding and spraying it makes an exceptional little garden rose: it was rated as "excellent" by the American Rose Society.

OVERALL ASSESSMENT **	FRAGRANCE ***
STRAIN —	BREEDING 'THE KNIGHT' × HT 'CHÂTEAU DE CLOS VOUGEOT'
APPELLATION —	DATE OF INTRODUCTION 1982

Prospero
← 4ft (120cm) →
3ft (90cm)

RECOMMENDED GROUPING 3–5

Queen Nefertiti

A very free-flowering rose with excellent repeat-flowering properties, QUEEN NEFERTITI is a tough and reliable variety. The blooms are of medium size, soft yellow in color and of rosette shape. They have a tendency to become tinged with pink in hot sunlight – just as we find in the Hybrid Tea 'Peace' – and this rather mars their appearance. At their best they have considerable beauty, but overall they fall short of the highest standards we set for the English Roses.

OVERALL ASSESSMENT *	FRAGRANCE **
STRAIN —	BREEDING 'LILIAN AUSTIN' × 'TAMORA'
APPELLATION AUSAP	DATE OF INTRODUCTION 1988

Redouté (BELOW)

This is a soft pink sport of the excellent MARY ROSE, which is of a much stronger shade. The description of MARY ROSE applies equally to REDOUTÉ, as the two roses differ only in color. In fact, REDOUTÉ is to my mind the more beautiful rose – it is as though the softness of its color changes its whole character, giving it something of the delicate charm of an old Alba Rose. Pierre-Joseph Redouté (1759–1840) was the most famous of all rose painters. His water colors included some 170 varieties from the collection of roses in the Empress Joséphine's garden at Malmaison.

OVERALL ASSESSMENT ***	FRAGRANCE *
STRAIN 'MARY ROSE'	BREEDING SPORT FROM 'MARY ROSE'
APPELLATION AUSPALE	DATE OF INTRODUCTION 1992

REDOUTÉ

St Cecilia (ABOVE)

ST CECILIA is an ideal English Rose where space is limited, for it manages to be both short and elegant at the same time. It bears its nicely cupped flowers widely spaced in open sprays; the stems are slightly arching so that the flowers bend forward to reach out to you in the most pleasing manner. The flowers are of medium size and pale buff-apricot turning almost white – a more attractive shade than words might convey. The combination of poise of flower and elegance of growth make it an excellent garden plant. Its foliage is not very plentiful, but is in just the right quantity to complement the general character of the rose. It has an unusually powerful myrrh fragrance. Unfortunately, it may be vulnerable to rust in certain districts where it would then require spraying.

OVERALL ASSESSMENT ***	FRAGRANCE ***
STRAIN 'WIFE OF BATH'	BREEDING 'WIFE OF BATH' × SEEDLING
APPELLATION AUSMIT	DATE OF INTRODUCTION 1987

St Swithun

ST SWITHUN bears large and beautiful flowers of slightly cupped rosette shape. Later the petals fall back a little to form a slightly domed flower. The color is soft pink, becoming paler towards the edges. The whole impression is one of great delicacy and softness. It has a delicious fragrance. The growth is of medium height, broad and bushy, with the flowers displayed to perfection above ample foliage. It is vigorous and disease-free.

St Swithun (b. 852 AD), after whom this rose is named, is the patron saint of Winchester Cathedral. According to legend, the weather conditions – be they wet or fine – on July 15, his Feast Day, will continue for the next forty days.

OVERALL ASSESSMENT ***	FRAGRANCE ***
STRAIN 'MARY ROSE'	**BREEDING** 'MARY ROSE' × ('CHAUCER' × RUGOSA 'CONRAD FERDINAND MEYER')
APPELLATION —	**DATE OF INTRODUCTION** 1993

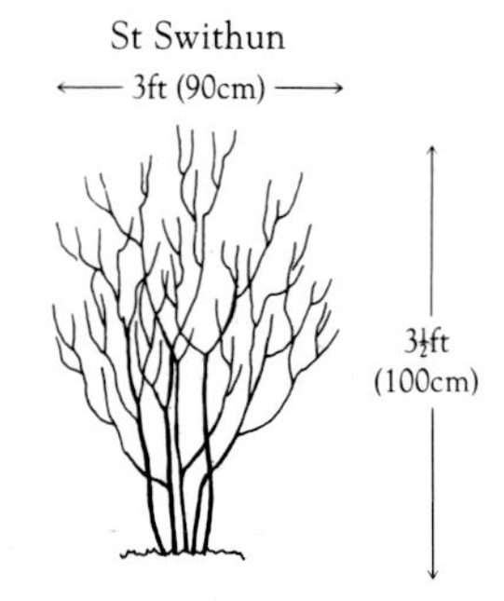

RECOMMENDED GROUPING 3

Sharifa Asma (ABOVE RIGHT)

This is an English Rose of rare delicacy and beauty; the flowers are the quintessence of all that I consider an Old Rose should be. They incurve in a rosette formation, soft pink in color with a touch of gold at the base of the petals; the outside petals are paler. Inside, the smaller petals twist attractively and there is sometimes a suggestion of a button-eye. The whole

SHARIFA ASMA

RECOMMENDED GROUPING 3

flower has a gentle translucent quality which is most appealing. Its growth is quite strong and bushy. There is a delicious fragrance. SHARIFA ASMA was bred from a cross between MARY ROSE and ADMIRED MIRANDA, an early English Rose with flowers of great beauty but an absence of vigor (it has since been taken off our list). SHARIFA ASMA combines the best points of both its parents.

OVERALL ASSESSMENT ***	FRAGRANCE ***
STRAIN 'WIFE OF BATH'	**BREEDING** 'MARY ROSE' × 'ADMIRED MIRANDA'
APPELLATION AUSREEF	**DATE OF INTRODUCTION** 1989

RECOMMENDED GROUPING 3 or more

OVERALL ASSESSMENT *	FRAGRANCE ***
STRAIN 'ALOHA'	BREEDING 'LILIAN AUSTIN' × 'CHAUCER'
APPELLATION —	DATE OF INTRODUCTION 1985

Sir Walter Raleigh (LEFT)

SIR WALTER RALEIGH produces some of the largest and most generous flowers to be found among the English Roses, but does so without any hint of coarseness. Rather like a tree peony, the numerous petals open wide to show a large boss of stamens. The color is a beautiful and pure shade of soft, glowing pink, and there is a strong and pleasing Old Rose fragrance. In spite of all these virtues, this rose has never proved as successful with us as we had hoped, making rather inadequate growth – although it does well in the US. It is a variety that needs to be planted in a group. It has some inclination to rust in areas where this is prevalent. It was named to mark the 400th anniversary of the founding of the first English-speaking colony in America.

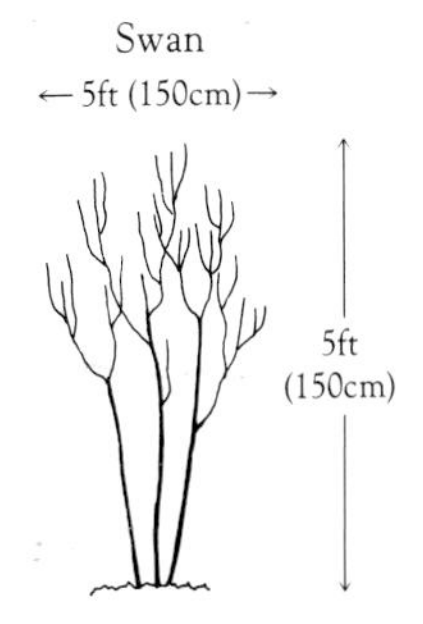

RECOMMENDED GROUPING 3–5

Swan

The white counterpart of the pink CLAIRE ROSE, SWAN has the same extra large, flat rosette-shaped flowers and tall, very strong, upright growth. The white of the flower is frequently tinged with buff and can be superb, particularly in warm, dry weather; in rain they tend to spot. It is a very suitable rose for the back of the border. The large, shiny leaves are modern in appearance. It has a moderate fragrance and was rated as "excellent" by the American Rose Society.

OVERALL ASSESSMENT *	FRAGRANCE *
STRAIN 'ALOHA'	BREEDING 'CHARLES AUSTIN' × (SEEDLING × FLORIBUNDA 'ICEBERG')
APPELLATION AUSWHITE	DATE OF INTRODUCTION 1987

Tamora
← 2ft (60cm) →
2½ft (75cm)

RECOMMENDED GROUPING 3–5

Sweet Juliet

This rose has dainty, small buds opening to rosette-shaped blooms of pure apricot, usually with a distinct button-eye. It has a strong "Tea Rose" fragrance. The foliage is very plentiful and attractive – long, pointed and elegant, and light green in color with an almost brownish tinge. It has an upright habit, providing an almost columnar effect, and is extremely robust. In fact, it is so vigorous that it produces a large number of shoots from the base and elsewhere, resulting in a thicket of growth often at the expense of flowers. This variety requires time before it shows its true value.

OVERALL ASSESSMENT ***	FRAGRANCE ***
STRAIN 'GLOIRE DE DIJON'	BREEDING 'GRAHAM THOMAS' × 'ADMIRED MIRANDA'
APPELLATION AUSLEAP	DATE OF INTRODUCTION 1989

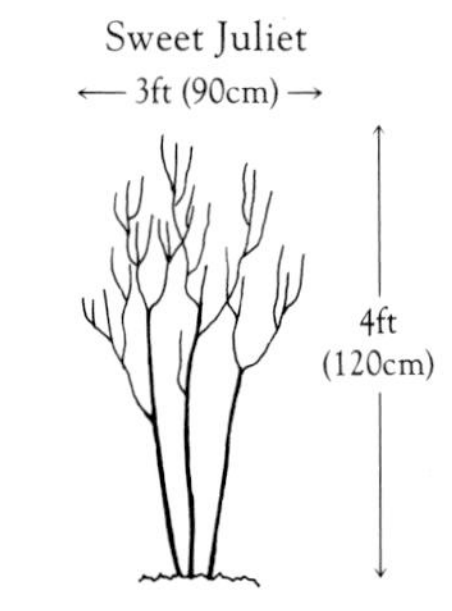

RECOMMENDED GROUPING 2–3

Tamora (LEFT)

The source of many of our best yellow roses, TAMORA was the result of one of our original crosses with the giant Rugosa 'Conrad Ferdinand Meyer.' Despite its parents, however, it forms a surprisingly short and upright bush with most flower stems coming from the base. Its blooms, of delicate apricot coloring, are shallowly cupped and have a strong myrrh fragrance. TAMORA is useful as a short-growing variety for the front of a border or for smaller gardens and makes an ideal bedding rose. It is remarkably disease-resistant.

OVERALL ASSESSMENT **	FRAGRANCE ***
STRAIN 'GLOIRE DE DIJON'	BREEDING 'CHAUCER' × RUGOSA 'CONRAD FERDINAND MEYER'
APPELLATION —	DATE OF INTRODUCTION 1983

The Alexandra Rose (BELOW)

though not usually classified as an English Rose, n including this variety since via its SHROPSHIRE S parent it is a descendant of an Alba Rose, and shows up strongly in its growth and foliage. The ers are quite small and single and are produced in abundance, repeating well later in the season. have a freshness and daintiness that I think puts t mong the best of the single-flowered garden r Their color is a coppery pink with a pale yellow ce the picture is completed by the airy stamens. Th wth is robust and healthy, making it an excellent garden shrub. It was named for the Alexandra Rose Day charity which raises money in Britain for various voluntary organizations.

OVERALL ASSESSMENT ***	FRAGRANCE *
STRAIN —	BREEDING ('SHROPSHIRE LASS' × 'SHROPSHIRE LASS') × 'HERITAGE'
APPELLATION AUSDAY	DATE OF INTRODUCTION 1992

The Alexandra Rose

RECOMMENDED GROUPING 1, 3 or more

The Countryman

This is one of my favorites. Like GERTRUDE JEKYLL, it is the result of a back-cross to an old Portland Rose. The flowers are less heavy and more dainty than those of GERTRUDE JEKYLL, the rather narrow petals contributing to their character and charm. The flowers form a slightly domed rosette and are a glowing, clear pink. They have a strong "Old Rose" fragrance.

THE COUNTRYMAN begins by growing upright, but the branches may later fall outwards, in the manner of LILIAN AUSTIN, to form an attractively spreading bush. As it is sometimes rather undecided in this habit, it is a good idea to encourage it by pegging down some of the branches with a hooked piece of wire pushed into the ground. It will then send out further branches with more flowers and build up into an excellent small shrub. The foliage is long and the leaflets widely separated as in Damask Roses. This rose received a "good" rating from the American Rose Society.

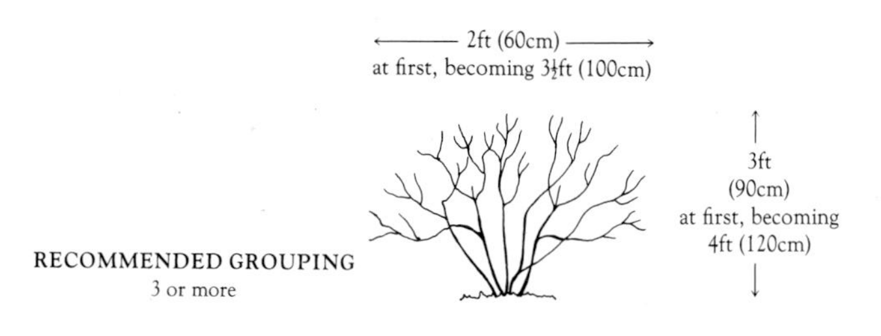

OVERALL ASSESSMENT ***	FRAGRANCE ***
STRAIN 'PORTLAND'	BREEDING 'LILIAN AUSTIN' × PORTLAND ROSE 'COMTE DE CHAMBORD'
APPELLATION AUSMAN	DATE OF INTRODUCTION 1979

The Dark Lady

THE DARK LADY has lovely, dusky crimson blooms which, like those of SIR WALTER RALEIGH, always remind me of the tree peonies one finds in the designs of Chinese fabrics. The flowers are large and somewhat informal in character, opening flat and then recurving a little. They have a strong "Old Rose" fragrance. The growth is adequately, but not excessively, strong and seems ideally suited to the flower; it spreads out broadly with dark green foliage. This rose takes its name from the "Dark Lady" of Shakespeare's sonnets.

OVERALL ASSESSMENT ***	FRAGRANCE ***
STRAIN 'THE SQUIRE'	BREEDING 'MARY ROSE' × 'PROSPERO'
APPELLATION AUSBLOOM	DATE OF INTRODUCTION 1991

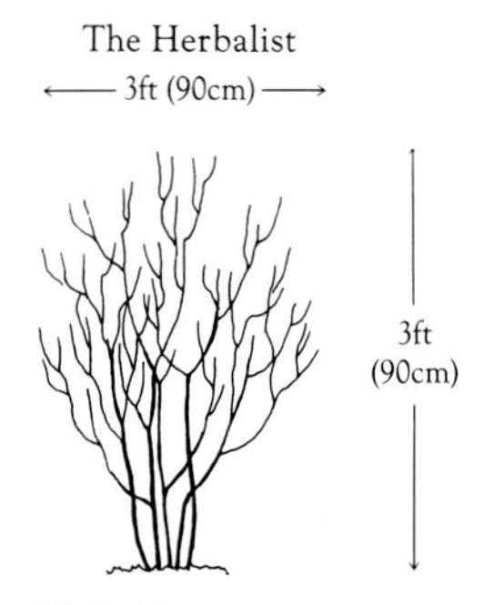

RECOMMENDED GROUPING 2, 3 or more

OVERALL ASSESSMENT **	FRAGRANCE *
STRAIN —	**BREEDING** SEEDLING × BOURBON ROSE 'LOUISE ODIER'
APPELLATION AUSSEMI	**DATE OF INTRODUCTION** 1991

The Herbalist (ABOVE)

We named this rose THE HERBALIST for its similarity to *R. gallica officinalis*, also known as the 'Apothecary's Rose,' and a rose of great antiquity. The flowers are semi-double, of a deep pink or light crimson color, opening flat with exposed, golden stamens; the growth is rather broad, low and bushy. The likeness to *R. gallica officinalis* is by no means exact, however, for THE HERBALIST repeat-flowers intermittently throughout the summer. Though neither particularly showy nor stylish, the blooms are produced with great freedom, providing an excellent effect in the garden. It is in fact an ideal rose for a mixed border and, like *R. gallica officinalis*, makes an effective edging plant.

The Miller (RIGHT)

A hybrid of the old Hybrid Perpetual 'Baroness Rothschild,' THE MILLER forms a very hardy and vigorous shrub with continual bloom. It will grow to a height of 6ft (1.8m) if permitted, but can be pruned down to make a smaller shrub; I have seen THE MILLER clipped to form an attractive hedge of about 4ft (1.2m). Its clear pink flower is double, sometimes almost semi-double, opening to show its stamens. This variety was one of our earlier introductions and the flowers are not quite of the quality we would expect today; however, at their best they can be most pleasing. Since this rose is tough and hardy, it is particularly suitable for seaside gardens.

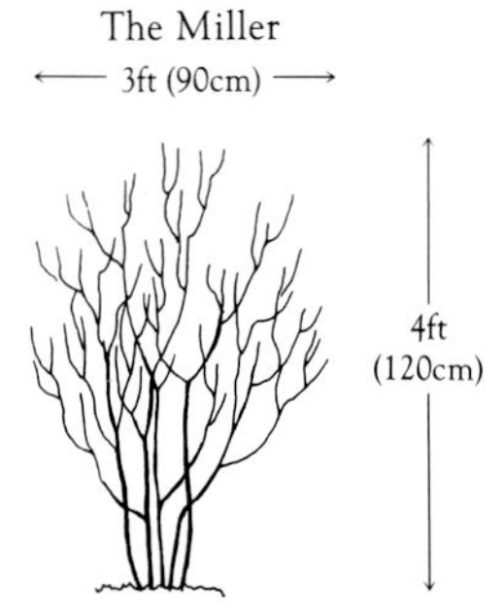

RECOMMENDED GROUPING 1–3

THE MILLER

The Nun (BELOW)

Though modest in character, as befits its name, THE NUN is a beautiful rose. Its flowers, a little more than medium-sized, are almost pure white and deeply cupped in shape, with a bunch of golden stamens at the base. Varieties with this type of flower frequently have a few small petals covering or partially covering the stamens, but in this rose we usually have a completely clean cup, which can be most appealing. The growth is rather open with slender and fairly large, somewhat sparse foliage. The blooms are nicely poised in wide sprays and open in succession.

OVERALL ASSESSMENT **	FRAGRANCE *
STRAIN 'HERITAGE'	BREEDING 'THE PRIORESS' × SEEDLING
APPELLATION —	DATE OF INTRODUCTION 1987

THE NUN

The Nun
3ft (90cm)
4ft (120cm)
RECOMMENDED GROUPING 3

OVERALL ASSESSMENT *	FRAGRANCE *
STRAIN 'OLD ROSE'	BREEDING HYBRID PERPETUAL 'BARONESS ROTHSCHILD' × 'CHAUCER'
APPELLATION —	DATE OF INTRODUCTION 1970

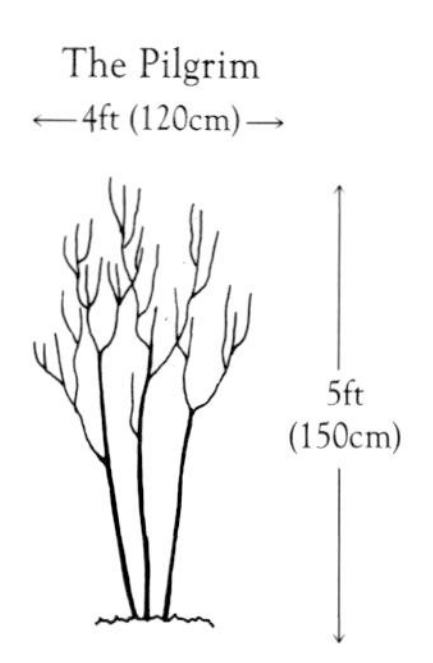

RECOMMENDED GROUPING 3 or more

The Pilgrim

This is one of the most reliable and beautiful of the yellow English Roses. Often the yellow shades are rather harsh in color, and for this reason are difficult to place in the garden or house. There is no such problem with THE PILGRIM. Its lovely silky flowers are of the softest yellow and of perfect rosette shape, with a multitude of small petals that seem to enhance the general delicacy of the flower. The inner petals are pale yellow, the outer almost white. Despite its exquisite blooms, it is an extremely robust rose, growing and flowering very freely. It is upright in habit – perhaps a little too upright for perfection – and has shiny green leaves more characteristic of a modern rose.

The rose was no chance seedling. I had always felt that a cross between GRAHAM THOMAS and YELLOW BUTTON would produce a rose that had both beauty and vigor. Unfortunately, however, it was a difficult cross to make, as YELLOW BUTTON produces very little pollen and no seed. Only by taking pollen from hundreds of flowers could we obtain enough for breeding. Initial results failed to realize the potential of such a match, but we persevered over many years, and eventually a rose appeared that fulfilled my highest hopes. A rose as good as THE PILGRIM is an all too rare reminder that the many years of work are worthwhile.

OVERALL ASSESSMENT ***	FRAGRANCE **
STRAIN —	BREEDING 'GRAHAM THOMAS' × 'YELLOW BUTTON'
APPELLATION AUSWALKER	DATE OF INTRODUCTION 1991

The Prince
3ft (90cm)
2½ft (75cm)
RECOMMENDED GROUPING 3–5

The Prince

THE PRINCE is a rose of superb coloring, opening as the deepest, richest crimson and quickly turning to a magnificent and equally rich royal purple. This latter shade is, I think, unique among Modern Roses; indeed, Graham Thomas believed THE PRINCE to be the first variety of this shade to be introduced since 1840. It is the type of purple we find among the old Gallicas, and wholly different from the typical metallic lilac of other Modern Roses. There is, as one would expect of such a rose, a powerful "Old Rose" fragrance. The flower is of true rosette formation, finishing slightly domed.

This rose takes its color from THE SQUIRE and its growth from LILIAN AUSTIN; in common with many seedlings from the latter, it has a low, spreading habit that is particularly useful at the edge of a border. The foliage is dark and modern in character. While a little more vigor would be desirable (something one could say of many other deep crimson roses), THE PRINCE is not a weak-growing variety.

OVERALL ASSESSMENT ***	FRAGRANCE ***
STRAIN 'ALOHA'	BREEDING 'LILIAN AUSTIN' × 'THE SQUIRE'
APPELLATION AUSVELVET	DATE OF INTRODUCTION 1990

The Reeve (BELOW)

This is a unique and unusual rose with flowers of deep globular shape, the petals incurving to such a degree that they sometimes almost meet at the center. They are of the darkest pink imaginable. Inside the flower, which is quite large, the golden stamens are visible. There is a strong "Old Rose" fragrance. The duskiness of THE REEVE's flowers is matched by dark green foliage, and together they give the whole plant a muted, soft-hued appearance; but this only seems to heighten the rose's attractions, particularly when it is placed with varieties of complementary coloring.

Growth is long and gracefully arching, with small sharp thorns. This is very much a rose for group planting, when its growth can entangle to form a single mass. It might look well planted where it could be encouraged to hang over a low retaining wall.

OVERALL ASSESSMENT **	FRAGRANCE ***
STRAIN 'OLD ROSE'	BREEDING 'LILIAN AUSTIN' × 'CHAUCER'
APPELLATION —	DATE OF INTRODUCTION 1979

RECOMMENDED GROUPING 3 or more

RECOMMENDED GROUPING 3–5

The Squire (ABOVE)

No other red rose that I know produces flowers of such superb Old Rose quality as THE SQUIRE. They are large, deeply cupped, and of the richest and deepest crimson, which gradually turns to a lovely rich purple. They also have an exceptionally powerful "Old Rose" fragrance. Here, sadly, the virtues end, for this variety has unusually sparse, open and stick-like growth; it also suffers from blackspot, which can leave it looking very bare. This is not, I hasten to add, the experience of all growers – many have bushes that perform excellently, so it may be concluded that much depends on the particular locality where they are grown. Those who are prepared to put up with these potential weaknesses, and perform the necessary spraying, will be rewarded with blooms of truly outstanding beauty. The foliage is thick, rough and dark green; there are many thorns.

OVERALL ASSESSMENT *	FRAGRANCE ***
STRAIN 'THE SQUIRE'	BREEDING 'THE KNIGHT' × HT 'CHÂTEAU DE CLOS VOUGEOT'
APPELLATION —	DATE OF INTRODUCTION 1977

Troilus

This variety, I am sure, would give its best results in warm, dry climates. When grown under glass in Britain, it produces magnificent, large globe-shaped blooms of honey-buff coloring. When grown outside, the blooms are tighter, smaller and less shapely. The growth is vigorous, sending up long flower stems with large leaves. It has a sweet fragrance.

OVERALL ASSESSMENT *	FRAGRANCE ***
STRAIN 'ALOHA'	BREEDING (GALLICA 'DUCHESSE DE MONTEBELLO' × 'CHAUCER') × 'CHARLES AUSTIN'
APPELLATION —	DATE OF INTRODUCTION 1983

Troilus
←3ft (90cm)→

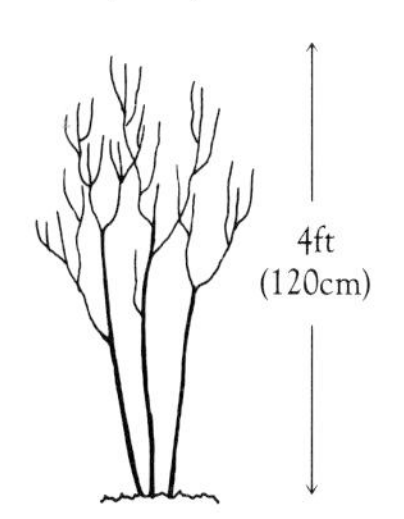

RECOMMENDED GROUPING 3

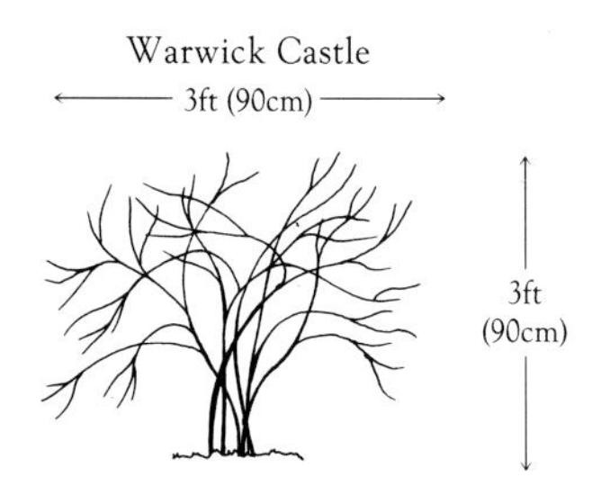

RECOMMENDED GROUPING 3

Warwick Castle

The result of a cross between LILIAN AUSTIN and THE REEVE, WARWICK CASTLE has inherited its attractive habit of growth from both its parents. It is neater than either, its arching stems forming a shapely mound, and this quality makes it an admirable plant for the front of a border. The individual flower is just as pleasing: it is a glowing pink color and its numerous, perfectly placed petals form a domed rosette. They have a delicious fragrance. This is an excellent little shrub, though there is a very slight tendency to blackspot. Its name commemorates the opening of the beautiful Victorian rose garden at Warwick Castle in 1986 on the site of the original garden (designed by Robert Marnock in 1868).

OVERALL ASSESSMENT *	FRAGRANCE ***
STRAIN —	BREEDING 'LILIAN AUSTIN' × 'THE REEVE'
APPELLATION AUSLIAN	DATE OF INTRODUCTION 1986

Wenlock (ABOVE)

Red roses, whether Hybrid Teas, English Roses or in any other group, have a tendency to be poor growers; or where a variety does have good growth, it is often the case that there is little fragrance. WENLOCK has the merit of being a very strong and reliable plant, which at its best produces some good crimson flowers with a strong "Old Rose" fragrance; although occasionally the color is a little dull. It is an excellent border rose, making a good show and repeating well. It has handsome, large, disease-free foliage and received a "good" rating from the American Rose Society.

OVERALL ASSESSMENT **	FRAGRANCE ***
STRAIN —	BREEDING 'THE KNIGHT' × 'GLASTONBURY'
APPELLATION —	DATE OF INTRODUCTION 1984

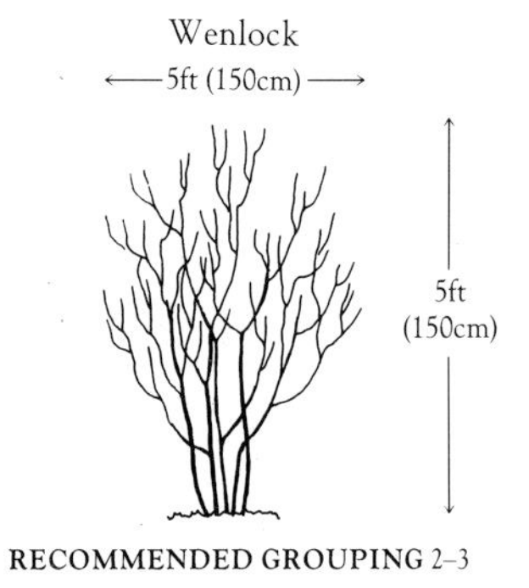

RECOMMENDED GROUPING 2–3

Wife of Bath (RIGHT)

This is one of our original English Roses. It is a short, tough and bushy little rose, whose only fault is a tendency to die-back in some of its branches. Despite this (and the branches can simply be removed), it is an almost indestructible rose. I know of one occasion when a garden was allowed to become overgrown, and the rose was buried in the grass for two or three years. It still survived after several cuttings with a mower, and eventually formed a good bush again.

The flowers of WIFE OF BATH are medium-sized, pink, and of cupped formation. They might be said to lack definition, being of rather informal shape, but they are nonetheless very attractive. They have a light myrrh fragrance.

OVERALL ASSESSMENT **	FRAGRANCE *
STRAIN 'WIFE OF BATH'	**BREEDING** HT 'MME CAROLINE TESTOUT' × (FLORIBUNDA 'MA PERKINS' × 'CONSTANCE SPRY')
APPELLATION —	**DATE OF INTRODUCTION** 1969

William Shakespeare

(ABOVE)

WILLIAM SHAKESPEARE bears attractive Gallica-like flowers of rosette form, in rich crimson quickly turning to purple, violet and mauve. The flowers can sometimes be a little dull, but more often they are comparable to the most superb Gallica Rose blooms.

Sadly, this rose has not turned out to be quite worthy of its illustrious name. Although its growth is exceptionally strong, it has developed a tendency to rust and blackspot which excludes it from the first rank of English Roses. In all other respects, it is a fine rose with a rich "Old Rose" fragrance.

OVERALL ASSESSMENT *	FRAGRANCE ***
STRAIN 'THE SQUIRE'	BREEDING 'THE SQUIRE' × 'MARY ROSE'
APPELLATION AUSROYAL	DATE OF INTRODUCTION 1987

Winchester Cathedral

A sport from MARY ROSE, to which it is identical in every way except in color, WINCHESTER CATHEDRAL is one of the best of the white varieties. The white flowers, sometimes showing a slight tinge of yellow at the center later in the season, are second only to those of GLAMIS CASTLE, a much shorter rose. It was named on behalf of the Winchester Cathedral Trust, in aid of the restoration of the Cathedral. For full details of its growth and habit, see MARY ROSE.

OVERALL ASSESSMENT ***	FRAGRANCE *
STRAIN 'MARY ROSE'	BREEDING SPORT FROM 'MARY ROSE'
APPELLATION AUSCAT	DATE OF INTRODUCTION 1988

Wise Portia

This rose is typical of some of our earlier varieties. At its best, it produces some of the most superbly beautiful flowers in a glorious, rich harmony of purples and mauves, reminiscent of the old Gallica Roses. Large and deeply cupped in formation, the flowers are carried on a rather small bush. They tend, however, to be extremely variable in color and are sometimes of rather duller hue. The growth is not quite as vigorous as that of our later varieties of English Roses. This rose is well worth growing and should respond to a generous treatment of fertilizers, as well as to regular spraying. The American Rose Society rates it as "excellent."

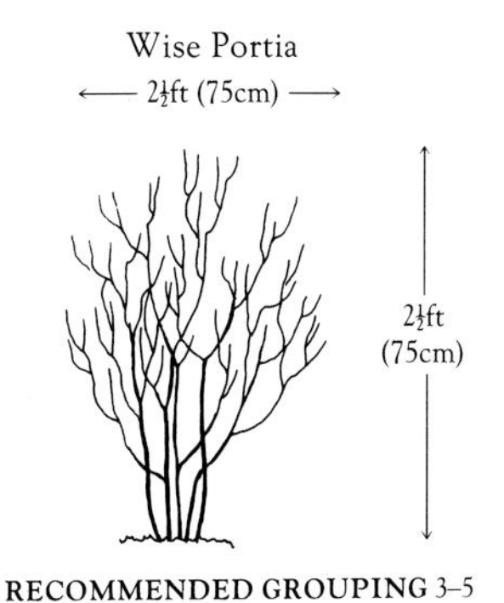

RECOMMENDED GROUPING 3–5

OVERALL ASSESSMENT *	FRAGRANCE ***
STRAIN —	BREEDING 'THE KNIGHT' × 'GLASTONBURY'
APPELLATION —	DATE OF INTRODUCTION 1982

YELLOW BUTTON

Yellow Button
3ft (90cm)
3ft
(90cm)

RECOMMENDED GROUPING 2–3

Yellow Button (ABOVE RIGHT)

One of our earliest introductions, and the first yellow variety of English Rose, its flowers are of good rosette shape, and its light yellow coloring has an occasional streak of yolk-yellow towards the center of the bloom. Its spreading habit of growth makes it a useful shrub for the front of the border. The foliage is shiny and light green in color.

OVERALL ASSESSMENT *	FRAGRANCE **
STRAIN —	BREEDING 'WIFE OF BATH' × FLORIBUNDA 'CHINATOWN'
APPELLATION —	DATE OF INTRODUCTION 1975

THE CULTIVATION OF ENGLISH ROSES

The cultivation of English Roses makes many of the same demands on the gardener as that of other roses. It is very easy to give the impression that it is a difficult and complicated subject, but this is by no means the case. Looking after your roses takes a little time and trouble, but requires no specialized knowledge or skill. There are, however, certain important differences which apply especially to the cultivation of English Roses.

The instructions given in this chapter are in the nature of a counsel of perfection. If you are not a particularly keen gardener but simply like the surroundings of your house to look attractive, any strong variety, given minimum attention, will still perform adequately and give much pleasure. Nonetheless, a little extra attention will give vastly improved results and consequently even greater satisfaction.

SITE AND SOIL PREPARATION

The choice of site is important. The first rule is not to choose for new roses any position where roses have been grown in the recent past: this will almost certainly have what is generally known as "rose-sickness" or "specific replant disease" – that is to say, there will be a build-up of soil organisms unfriendly to roses. The most likely culprit is rose eel-worm (nematode), although other factors may be involved. Rose-sickness may persist over a number of years, so it is advisable not to plant in a vulnerable piece of ground for at least five years. However, many people have a place in their garden where they have always grown roses and would like to continue to do so, or they may have a rose garden or border that they want to replant with new roses. There are ways that this can be done. Rose-sickness is very localized and if your planting can be moved to one side of the place occupied by the previous rose, the results should be satisfactory. Failing this, you can remove the soil to a depth of 1ft (30cm), and replace it with "clean" soil from elsewhere in the garden. In either case, always dig in plenty of humus in the form of rotted manure or garden compost: large quantities of humus have been shown to set up vigorous bacterial action in the soil, which restores the balance between harmful and beneficial soil organisms.

'Gertrude Jekyll' is a good example of the strongest-growing varieties of English Rose, with large Old Rose-type blooms and an exceptionally strong fragrance.

Where a larger area is to be replanted with roses, it may be worth considering soil sterilization by the use of a soil fumigant. Most chemicals for this purpose are not recommended for use by amateurs, and the fumigation must be carried out by a professional; many landscape gardeners will provide this service.

Another frequent cause of failure, particularly for English Roses and for other roses that are repeat-flowering, is competition from the roots of neighboring trees, hedges and shrubs. These roses need plenty of room round them to supply the necessary food and moisture for their recurrent habit.

Any reasonably good garden soil is suitable for English Roses. Before planting, always dig in liberal quantities of farmyard manure, compost, leaf-mold or other humus-based fertilizers, such as those supplied by garden centers under various brand names; the results will be greatly improved. The original ancestors of most garden roses were shrubs flourishing in humus-rich soil. Here, I am sure, lies the secret of successful rose growing.

Poor limy or very light sandy soils present more of a problem, but by no means an insuperable one. Here again, the answer lies in ample supplies of humus, which in these soils becomes not just desirable but essential. It is also worthwhile buying a planting mixture from a garden center to use in the hole dug out for your rose. Alternatively, you can prepare a good mixture of your own, with rich soil and well-rotted compost or manure. It is difficult to overdo the amount of humus you give English Roses, provided that it is well mixed in, for, as I have stressed before, all repeat-flowering roses have a big task in the production of flowers throughout the summer.

Roses enjoy a very slight acidity in the soil, about 6.5 on the pH scale: anything more acid than this would require a dressing of limestone, but be careful not to use this in excess. A dressing of peat moss will help to increase the acidity, as will leaf-mold. Drainage is also important, as roses do not like to have their roots standing in water-logged conditions: soggy areas should therefore be avoided.

Roses generally thrive in a sunny site, and no rose will tolerate more than very light shade in the morning or early evening.

PLANTING

The roots of the rose should be spread out in a hole of adequate width and depth – about 12–18in (30–40cm) deep – and the bush placed at a depth to cover the point where the roots meet the green top growth: the point at which the rose was budded on the root stock. In milder climates the graft can be above the soil surface. The soil conditions at the time of planting should be moist, but not too wet as there is a danger that the soil will compact into an airless mass. In these circumstances, a planting mixture can be used, placed immediately around the roots. Alternatively, look for a little dry soil to be found around walls and in other places and use this, mixed perhaps with a little peat. The soil around the plant should be well "firmed" in – not so firm as to be hard, but firm enough to hold the rose securely in place.

I would like to reiterate here the importance I attach to group planting for English Roses as well as for other repeat-flowering Shrub Roses. Groups of two, three or more bushes of any one variety are best planted in fairly close proximity to each other – perhaps no more than 18–24in (50–60cm) apart – so that they grow together to form a thicket of growth. In this way, you will get a marvelous concentration of flowers, and achieve the effect of a single plant. Varieties vigorous enough to be planted singly need generous spacing, perhaps 3ft (90cm) to 5ft (150cm).

PRUNING

There are no hard and fast rules that can be applied to the pruning of all the different classes of Shrub Roses, as there are to the pruning of the Hybrid Teas and Floribundas. This is because Shrub Roses are very diverse in their habits of growth; some are small, and others very large. It is, however, a little easier to lay down rather more specific guidelines for pruning the English Roses.

English Roses are best pruned in the early days of winter – perhaps in late November or December in mild areas. In the North (Zones 4–7), wait until early to mid spring. This gives them a chance to shoot early.

GROUP PLANTING

To produce the very best effect with English Roses, I strongly recommend planting several plants of one variety closely in a group. The plants will grow together to produce the effect of one strongly growing and floriferous shrub.

ABOVE *Plant in groups of three or five, as odd numbers give the most natural-looking effect. Space the plants more closely than normal: a distance of 18in (50cm) is ideal.* RIGHT *The plants will quickly grow together.*

SUPPORTING ROSES

A way to encourage English Roses to form a freely flowering, arching mound is to tie the stems to an encircling rail about 18in (45cm) high. The rose will produce flowers all along the length of its stems. Suitable varieties: 'Abraham Darby,' 'Cymbeline,' 'English Elegance,' 'Golden Celebration' and 'Jayne Austin.'

PEGGING ROSES

Pegging rose stems to the ground using short lengths of bent wire was a technique widely used by the Victorians on the old Hybrid Perpetuals. As with the rail (above) the rose is encouraged to shoot all along the length of its stems. English Roses with growth flexible enough for this method are 'Charmian,' 'Lilian Austin,' 'Lucetta' and 'The Reeve.'

Early pruning seems to bring the whole season forward so that this last crop can occur in good time. Many gardeners believe that pruning roses at this time runs the risk of them being damaged by early frosts, but very rarely is any harm done.

Some nurseries now ship English Roses prepruned, so no pruning (except for the removal of damaged growth) is needed in the first year. In subsequent years, our overall advice is that, where you are looking for smaller plants with larger, better quality flowers, the shoots should be reduced by half their length. If you want a larger shrub with more flowers, we advise cutting back the individual shoots by one-third. Shorter pruning diverts the strength of the plant into producing fewer flowers, which will as a result be larger and finer. These are only very general rules which should be modified according to the nature of the variety and the function you wish it to fulfill – for example, as a tall plant, a broad bush, or whatever. Remove any small, weak shoots completely, as these will seldom produce flowers. Similarly, take out any growth that shows signs of disease or decay. As the years go by, older wood can be removed from the base of the bush to make way for strong young shoots.

It is as well to bear in mind that pruning is as much an art as a craft. While some professional gardeners like to see their roses all shorn and clean and tidy after pruning, this is not always desirable. Due thought should be paid to the ultimate appearance of the plant as it will develop during the coming summer. There is no need to feel confined to the broad rules I have laid down above and opposite – they are intended to be broken where appropriate. Aim to build up interesting, shapely growth, whether bushy, arching or whatever else. Do not be inhibited from leaving extra branches where these may help the general appearance of the plant. This does not mean that pruning is unimportant – without the removal of some growth the plant will not be able to produce flowers of sufficient quality, nor will it repeat-flower adequately.

In the early stages of the shrub's life, the aim should be to establish the basic framework by removing small, spindly shoots and leaving strong shoots on which future growth can be built. This applies particularly to such varieties as 'Graham Thomas,' 'Heritage,' 'Brother Cadfael,' 'Lucetta' and 'Abraham Darby,' among others; these will be much more graceful in habit if a good framework has been achieved at the beginning.

With mature plants, much depends upon the natural growth of the individual variety. Some, like 'English Elegance,' 'The Reeve,' 'Lilian Austin,' 'Bibi Maizoon,' 'Lucetta' and 'Cymbeline,' have an elegant, arching habit. It is important that you do not remove too much wood from these roses or they will lose their width; at the same time, you should not allow them to become over-tall and ungainly. Where necessary, notes on their pruning will be found with the descriptions of the individual varieties. Stiff, upright roses, such as 'Financial Times Centenary,' 'Charles Austin' and 'Claire Rose,' may be allowed to grow upwards if they are placed at the back of the border; nearer the front they can be fairly hard pruned to stop them becoming leggy. Bushy, twiggy varieties, whether they be large or small, can be encouraged in their bushiness, but at the same time it is best to remove very weak growth so that the plant does not produce small flowers. 'Sweet Juliet' and 'Jayne Austin' are unusual in that they make so much growth that the bush cannot cope with it and some shoots fail to produce flowers. In these cases, it is particularly beneficial to reduce the amount of growth by removing sideshoots or whole stems.

The art of pruning English Roses, therefore, is largely a matter of achieving a balance between the quality of the flowers and the grace and shape of the bush itself. Usually, hard pruning obtains the former, light pruning the latter. There is no need, however, for the gardener to worry too much about this: pruning should be regarded as an interesting experiment to see what effect can be achieved. Experience will bring confidence and mastery.

Some of the shorter English Rose varieties make excellent bedding roses. For this purpose, they should be pruned as one would a Hybrid Tea: cut them back to about 5 or 6in (12 or 15cm) from the ground to get even growth throughout the bed. With some of the larger-scale English Roses, in larger beds, you can be less severe in your pruning, depending on the height you wish to achieve. Remember to remove weak and aging wood as usual and cut back winter-damaged shoots to live wood.

PRUNING ENGLISH ROSES

The chapter "Varieties of the English Rose" categorizes the growth of each variety as spreading, arching, bushy or upright. These notes offer general guidelines on how to prune each type. The job is best done in early winter (see page 146).

PRUNING SPREADING SHAPES

Remove about a third of the length of each stem, cutting to just above an outward-facing bud. Aim to maintain the natural width and spreading shape of the plant.

PRUNING ARCHING SHAPES

Prune lightly to maintain maximum height and width in these shapes. Prune back a fifth to a quarter of each stem, cutting to a bud.

PRUNING BUSHY SHAPES

Encourage the rose in its bushiness by pruning out about a third of the length of each stem, cutting to a bud each time; the buds will break and produce plenty of flowering growth. Remove any weak growth.

PRUNING UPRIGHT SHAPES

These forms can be hard pruned to stop them becoming leggy, by removing about half of the length of each stem. Cut to an outward-facing bud each time.

PRUNING FOR BEDDING

When English Roses are grown as bedding, prune as for a Hybrid Tea: cut each stem to an outward-facing bud about 6in (15cm) from the ground.

GENERAL MAINTENANCE

Once the roses have been pruned, prick the soil over lightly with a fork and put a dressing of rotted manure or other humus around the bushes. This will not be necessary in the first year, when ample supplies will already have been dug in. In subsequent years, there can be no doubt that the annual mulch of humus is extremely beneficial. Not only does it feed the plant, but it also helps to retain moisture.

When growth starts in the spring, apply a dressing of rose fertilizer. Apply a further dressing when the first flowers are well under way, to encourage growth for the next crop.

Without water, feeding will be of little use. Only in the presence of moisture can the various elements required for plant growth be taken up and used. Even in climates such as that of the British Isles, rain is seldom sufficient throughout the summer. Additional water, soaking the ground thoroughly each time, will give vastly improved results. In drier climates watering and irrigation become essential for roses.

DEAD-HEADING

Where time allows, the removal of flowers as they die is advisable. This not only makes the plant look much more tidy, but also encourages new growth. Some varieties, such as 'Peach Blossom,' produce a mass of hips if not dead-headed in this way. Once the rose produces hips it will not provide new growth nor new flowers, so whereas the hips can often be attractive, you will have to decide early on whether you would prefer to have them, or further flowers. Dead-heading is best done with a sharp pair of pruners and as soon as possible after the fading of the flowers.

PESTS AND DISEASES

Roses are not subject to many diseases, but those that do affect them can be a considerable nuisance. English Roses are no exception to this rule, although some varieties show greater resistance than others.

The three main diseases are mildew, rust and blackspot – the last being the worst offender. Mildew, which thrives in high-humidity areas, is easily controlled, and rust, though more difficult to control when it occurs, is not so prevalent. Prevention is, as always, better than cure. When you have completed the pruning, it is best to rake up as many of the fallen leaves as possible, as these may contain disease spores from the previous years which could be passed on.

Once growth begins, the customary advice would be to spray after rain or about every two weeks. You can use a general fungicide for this, but, despite manufacturers' claims, there is no fungicide that protects against all three diseases: most will deal with blackspot and mildew; others with a combination of rust and mildew. Whatever spray you choose to use, however, it is not essential to spray as often as the times quoted above. By spraying at the first appearance of the disease – perhaps followed by one further spray – you will achieve adequate protection, and only need to repeat this on its reappearance. It is important, however, never to allow disease to get a hold. Much will depend on how many roses there are in the vicinity. A garden full of roses will obviously have a greater potential for infection. Where there are only a few groups of roses spaced well apart, this is much less likely and spraying could be very limited or may even be unnecessary.

Pests in the form of insects are easier to deal with. The main problem is aphids. For these a systemic rose spray should be used. Sprays, both for the control of insects and diseases, can be purchased from a garden center and should be used strictly according to the manufacturers' instructions. Consult an Extension Specialist for help with local pest problems.

POTS AND CONTAINERS

English Roses grown in pots, tubs, urns or other containers can give much satisfaction, but a little extra care is needed in their preparation and general maintenance. In the first place, choose a container which is as large as practicable: not less than 15in (40cm) in diameter and 12in (25cm) in height. Make sure also that

Bushy and vigorous in growth, generous in its continuous production of blooms, 'Mary Rose' is both a fine example of the English Roses and a first-rate garden shrub.

it has adequate holes in the bottom for free drainage. The soil for the container will need to be a mixture that is both rich and easily drained. One based entirely on peat moss is unsuitable for roses. Instead, use a growing medium half of good garden soil and half of a standard synthetic soil mixture, such as Redi-Earth, Jiffy Mix, Pro-Mix, or a similar mix, available from garden centers. A standard rose fertilizer can be added to the medium. Using only soil in a container large enough for English Roses makes it too heavy to move about. General care is very much the same as for roses grown in open ground – with the following two vital provisos.

First, you should remember that roses in containers are, of course, entirely dependent on the water you provide for them. Falling rain will only dampen the soil to some small extent, and the pots do need to be kept watered at all times. The second point is that the roses will soon use up any nourishment that may be in their soil and will require regular applications of fertilizer. In using any fertilizer it is better to observe how the rose is growing than to adhere too closely to the directions provided by the manufacturer. Fertilizer helps to keep the plant growing well and produces good dark foliage; too much feeding can result in the plant becoming coarse and gross. You might begin by following the instructions and then adapt them according to how the rose is progressing.

There will come a time, after perhaps two or three years, when the rose is "pot-bound." You will then have to take the dormant rose, complete with its soil, out of its container and re-pot it, either in the same pot or in another. This involves removing some of its soil and replacing the plant in the pot with some rich new soil around it. In very cold zones outdoor potted roses need some protection over the winter.

English Roses grown in a conservatory or greenhouse should be given much the same treatment as outlined above. Pruning should be carried out in the autumn; then it would be best to allow the roses a period of dormancy by placing them outside for a few weeks in the winter. During the rest of the year, careful watering becomes even more essential under glass: even a short period of drought can be fatal for a rose.

SUMMING UP

Key points in the cultivation of English Roses:

1. Mix ample quantities of rotted manure or other humus in the soil before planting.
2. Plant in groups of two, three or more bushes of the same variety, to achieve a bushy effect.
3. Prune in early winter in mild zones, in early spring in the North, to half or three-quarters of the length of the shoot, after thinning out weak growth.
4. Mulch with rotted manure or other humus annually or every other year. Feed with rose fertilizer twice a year: in early spring and early summer.
5. Spray at the first sign of disease, especially after rain for blackspot and continue at intervals.
6. Remember that the roses marked *** under Overall Assessment (pages 78–143) usually prove to be the easiest varieties to grow.

Provided you follow these broad instructions, as well as of course using a liberal dash of common sense, the routine maintenance of your English Roses should present few problems. Properly looked after, they should repay you with years of enjoyment.

Creating a New Rose

I am often asked how a new rose is bred. To many people, the process of hybridization seems to have something slightly magical about it, as if it comes about by alchemy. The reality is, of course, much more mundane, but even after a lifetime of rose breeding, the subject still fascinates me.

For the uninitiated, I should first of all explain that most new roses are produced by a process of transferring pollen from one variety to another – in other words, "hybridization." The seed from this cross-fertilization is then sown and a variety of seedlings are produced, each of which will be unique. From these seedlings the best are selected and a new rose is born. This brief summary might give the impression that a new variety of English Rose can be created almost overnight. In fact, it is an elaborate exercise of elimination and selection, requiring thought, perseverance and patience.

The entire process, which takes a total of eight years or more, begins in the mind: very little can be achieved without a clear idea of what one is aiming for. Most of my winter evenings are spent working out the crosses that I shall be making the following summer – a long and complicated business, since the possible combinations are so numerous. It is important to be able to visualize the results that may be expected from a cross. This is done on the basis of knowledge gained from past experience. Over the years one gradually learns that certain roses have a potential for reproducing certain characteristics; in the absence of such knowledge, it is more a question of relying on the hope of a particular outcome in the new rose. In other words, careful study and good luck both play their parts.

Close inspection of every new seedling (left) is a vital part of the breeding and selection process. Observation and assessment goes on throughout the years of development.

At our nurseries, the hybridizing is done in a large greenhouse, where some 1,500 potted roses have been placed for the purpose. The greenhouse provides protection from wet weather, which might otherwise interfere with fertilization. It also ensures the ripening of the hips which, in our comparatively short, cool summers, may not be possible outdoors. The hybridizing work is carried out in May by eight members of our staff – fewer in cool weather when the flowers will open only slowly.

Pollination in any flower involves the transfer of pollen grains produced in the stamens (the "male" part of the flower) on to the stigma (see page 155). The pollen might be carried there by wind or insects. Once there, the pollen grains germinate and send down a pollen tube into the ovary of the flower. A nucleus in the pollen fuses with a nucleus contained inside the ovule. The now-fertilized egg divides and becomes an embryo, and the ovule becomes the seed that surrounds and protects it. The base of the flower swells and becomes the rose hip, the job of which is to ensure the dispersal of the seed by offering itself as food for animals and birds.

The rose breeder manipulates these natural processes to produce new varieties of rose. First the stamens of the flowers chosen as seed parents are removed on the day before hybridization, to avoid self-pollination (and hence self-fertilization) of the flower. At the same time, stamens from the roses chosen as the male parents are removed and placed in small dishes, each clearly labelled. There they are allowed to burst and release their pollen into the dish. The pollen is then transferred on to the stigma of the seed (female) parent, effecting a controlled cross-pollination that, all being well, will lead to a successful cross-fertilization. The cross is labeled on the plant and carefully recorded in a book.

Before long, the hips begin to swell and by September they are ripe and ready for removal from the plant. The seed is then taken from the hips and placed in cold storage to ensure that it has a period of "winter" conditions. By January the seed is ready for sowing in a propagating house. This is done in seed trays, where

These small, carefully labeled jars contain the stamens from the chosen pollen parents, which will burst overnight and provide the pollen for hybridization the following day.

When the first year seedlings bloom in the greenhouse, I use marker sticks to indicate those that should be retained for propagation by budding, and growing on outside.

germination will take place within a few weeks. The percentage that germinates is often comparatively low – some will not do so until the following year, many not at all. Germination is controlled by temperature, and as the year goes by and the days get warmer, it ceases. This is logical: the year would now be too advanced for the plant to develop well enough before the arrival of the winter cold, so nature calls a halt.

THE SEEDLINGS

When the seedlings are still quite small, they are transferred to a large greenhouse we call the "seedling house." There they are planted on benches in a peat mixture about 3in (8cm) apart. They soon begin to shoot and in as little as twelve weeks some of them will be showing flowers; others may take longer. This is the time when things become interesting, for now the first selection can be made. Each cross produces a great diversity of flowers and it is from this that we make our choice. It is not difficult to imagine the excitement of seeing thousands of little seedlings for the first time, each a few inches in height and carrying a small bloom. In spite of all the thought and planning, it is impossible to predict what is going to turn up: the next seedling could always be the one we are looking for. The seedlings have to be studied daily to avoid missing anything that might be significant.

At last, after much thought and selection, some 200 roses, out of the 50,000 seedlings that we started with, are passed along to what we call the multiplication area. Each rose represents a possible new variety. We now propagate the roses by budding again, to produce perhaps eighty plants of each. These roses undergo another two or three years of scrutiny, with regular assessments of their strength, beauty and other characteristics, as before. After this extended period, we hope to have five or six good roses that will form new varieties for commercial introduction.

THE SELECTED VARIETIES

The new varieties are now ready for propagation on a much larger scale. First we will produce 500 plants of each rose, and the following year we will increase these to 3–5,000. We then have enough stock to send out propagating material for growing roses on a commercial scale in our rose fields, and for eventual distribution to our customers.

Propagation material in the form of budding wood will also be sent out to some eighty British growers, who have the right to grow at least some of our latest varieties for their customers. Our European agents, as well as those in the United States, Canada, South Africa, Australia and New Zealand, will also receive budding wood, so that they can propagate the roses in their own trial grounds in order to assess their suitability for their particular climates. Many nurserymen visit our nursery and trial grounds each year, to see the new varieties at first hand. We also visit other countries to see how our roses are faring under different conditions, knowledge that we can put to use in our breeding program in the future.

Our new varieties are introduced each year at The Chelsea Flower Show, the highlight of the British horticultural year. As May comes around, it falls to me to find names for the new varieties, a task that is not always as easy as it seems. Naming is important and can affect the popularity of a rose, since the names very quickly become part and parcel of that rose's character. We often like to choose names with historic associations. 'Sir Walter Raleigh,' 'Warwick Castle' and 'Mary Rose' are examples. Or we may choose names from literature; our Shakespearian and Chaucerian choices have been some of our most successful ideas, such as 'Wife of Bath,' 'Perdita' and 'Prospero:' such names carry with them evocative associations that are exactly appropriate to the nature of our roses. Occasionally we will name a rose in association with another company or magazine, and usually each year we name a rose for charity, donating a small percentage of the profits from it. In 1992 it was 'The Alexandra Rose,' in aid of Alexandra Rose Day. Whatever the source, I am constantly on the look-out for promising names with appropriate connotations.

From my descriptions of how a rose is bred, selected, grown on and assessed, it can be seen that the whole process from hybridization to commercial introduction takes no less than eight years. People tend to gasp at the patience required, but there is always something new coming along each year to keep the interest and excitement alive. By the end of the eight-year period our chosen roses will have become old friends, and we feel that we know all about them, their virtues and their weaknesses. As with people, none is perfect in every respect, but they are always beautiful – of that I am sure. And after all, that is what really counts in rose breeding.

The shallowly cupped rosettes of 'Cottage Rose' are a pure, glowing pink. This is both a good garden rose and of true 'Old Rose' character, two features we value in our breeding program.

INDEX

SOURCES OF ENGLISH ROSES

The following is a selective list of suppliers of English Roses. Local garden centers may also offer some varieties.

Main agents, USA

Jackson & Perkins
1 Rose Lane
Medford
Oregon 97501-0702

Wayside Gardens
1 Garden Lane
Hodges
South Carolina 29695-0001

Main agent, Canada

Hortico
723 Robson Road R.R.#1
Waterdown
Ontario LOR 2H1
Catalog $3

Other sources

Country Bloomers Nursery
R.R.#2
Udall
Kansas 67146
Mostly own-root selected English and Old Roses

Forevergreen Farm
70 New Glouster Road
North Yarmouth
Maine 04097
Many English and Old Roses; catalog $1

Green's Flowers
8731 Bel Air Street
Buena Park
California 90620

Heirloom Old Garden Roses
24062 Riverside Drive N.E.
St. Paul
Oregon 97137
Large selection of own-root English Roses; catalog $5

Love's Own Root Roses
6 Sheffield Road
Nashua
New Hampshire
Selections of earliest English and Old Roses; catalog $2

Park Seed Company
Cotesbury Road
Greenwood
South Carolina 29647

Pickering Nurseries
670 Kingston Road
Pickering
Ontario LIV 1A6, Canada
Catalog $3

Roseraie At Bay Fields
Waldoboro
Maine 04572
Selections of English and Old Roses

Roses of Yesterday and Today, Inc.
Brown's Valley Road
Watsonville
California 95076
Selected early English Roses and Old and Modern Roses; catalog $3

Winterthur Museums and Gardens
Winterthur
Delaware 19735
Catalog $3

ACKNOWLEDGMENTS

Author's acknowledgments
I wish to express my thanks to a number of people who have helped in the production of this book: Anne Dakin, for giving me extensive help in writing the chapter on 'English Roses in the Home'; the editorial and design staff at Conran Octopus – in particular Sarah Riddell and Sarah Pearce, who edited this book; Diane Ratcliff, for typing the script and much other help relating to this book.

Photographic acknowledgments
All photographs were specially taken by Clay Perry except the following: 17 right Photos Horticultural; 18 Vincent Page; 24 top left Harry Smith; 25 below Photos Horticultural; 28 below David Austin.

The photographer and publisher would like to thank the following for their kind permission to photograph their gardens: Lord and Lady Carrington; Ms A. Chambers, Kiftsgate Court, Gloucestershire; Dr Robert Doyle, Carmel Valley, CA; Gary Fredericks and Joey Webb, Carpentera, CA; The Gardens of the Rose, St Albans, Hertfordshire; Ms Z. W. Grant, Kent; Mrs R. Green, Santa Barbara, CA; Mr and Mrs Herbert, Casa Pacifica, San Clemente, CA; Mottisfont Abbey, Hampshire; Ernest B. Schultz, Palos Verdes, CA; Ms F. L. Seton, Kent; Mrs B. Stockitt, The Show Gardens at West Kington Nurseries, Wiltshire; Sudeley Castle, Gloucestershire: designer Jane Fearnley-Whittingstall; Sharon Van Enoo, Torrance, CA.

Publisher's acknowledgments
The publishers would like to thank: Dan Bifano, Santa Barbara, CA; Prue Bucknall; Jane Chapman; Olwen Gaut; Holly Joseph, Santa Barbara, CA; Tony Lord; Barbara Mellor; Maggie Perry; Doreen Pike; Alistair Plumb; Caroline Taylor; Peggy Vance. The publishers would also like to thank all those whose gardens it was not in the end possible to photograph or include in the book.
Location research: George Galitzine, Maxine Harrison and Boots Scott (UK); Maureen Fulgoni (USA)
Index compiled by Indexing Specialists, Hove, East Sussex BN3 2DJ.